Combination Microwave Cookery

Carol Bowen has a degree in Home Economics from the University of Surrey. She has been a freelance cookery writer, food consultant and broadcaster since 1979, having previously worked for *Good Housekeeping*, *Homes & Gardens* and Birds Eye (as Head of Consumer Affairs). Carol has contributed frequently to national newspapers, magazines and radio programmes including a regular spot with Michael Aspel on Capital Radio and a cookery programme *What's Cooking* on Piccadilly Radio in Manchester. On television she was cookery consultant and guest on the X-Cel Diet for TV AM with Diana Dors and made a guest appearance on the BBC's *Snowdon on Camera* on food photography. To date she has written over forty cookery books including *Versatile Vegetables* (Octopus) which won the 1984 Bejam Cookery Book of the Year Award. She has a strong belief in and a passion for the microwave – a subject on which she advises the *Sunday Telegraph Magazine*. Carol Bowen is married and lives with her husband and two children in Surrey.

Other cookery books available in Pan

Carol Bowen

Combination Microwave Cookery

Pan Original
Pan Books London, Sydney and Auckland

First published 1988 by Pan Books Ltd,
Cavaye Place, London SW10 9PG
9 8 7 6 5 4 3
© Carol Bowen 1988
ISBN 0 330 30188 8

Phototypeset by Input Typesetting Ltd, London
Printed in Great Britain by
Richard Clay Ltd, Bungay, Suffolk

Contents

Acknowledgements

I should like to offer my grateful thanks to Sharp Electronics
(U.K.), Thorn EMI Domestic Appliances, Robert Bosch Ltd,
Bejam Ltd and Jones and Brother Ltd for kindly lending ovens
for testing purposes. For invaluable information on recipe
guidelines and timings thank the same companies and Toshiba
(U.K.) Ltd, Panasonic UK Ltd, Belling and Co. Ltd, Hitachi
Sales UK Ltd, Siemens Domestic Appliances and Neff (UK) Ltd.
    For information thank the Mushroom Grower's Association,
Colman Foods, The Danish Dairy Board, British Meat, Pasta
Information Centre, Danish Meat and Bacon Council, Cranberry
Information Bureau, Green Giant Kitchen, British Alcan
Consumer Products Ltd, Weight Watchers From Heinz, Gale's
Honey Bureau, The Other Sausage Bureau, Food and Wine
From France Ltd, Outspan, Total Yogurt and Kingdom Kitchen.

For Lucinda and Charles
who appreciate and love fine food

Foreword

The microwave revolution continues ... with the combination microwave oven – and as it does it unfolds and reveals the delights of many yesteryear traditional favourites. Long forgotten but always missed dishes like crispy golden pastry crowned pies, fluffy yet firm and brown baked soufflés, sizzling hot steamed gratins and no-need-to-disguise browned cakes, breads and other home-baked treats.

There is no doubt that the microwave has become one of the most exciting developments of the decade in the kitchen – making speedy and nutritious cooking a thing of today. I welcomed it with more than open arms some 12 years ago and skillfully manouevred around those little setbacks it had – namely lack of crisping and browning. Friends and family alike revelled at the way it came into and then dominated my cooking life. Imagine then my delight of news that manufacturer's were hard at work producing a microwave that would crisp and brown yet still cook food in the minutes and seconds I had come to expect.

And now here it is, the fruits of that intense development work – the combination microwave oven – in the shape of some twenty or more models all based on microwave with convection heat. I can faithfully say I have tested nearly all of them in the last eight years (yes, I tried perhaps the first domestic model back in 1979) and my enthusiasm has risen to new heights with the new developments, refinements and features now available. It is hardly surprising for here is a machine that will literally do everything your conventional oven can do, in often less than half the time, with the same results, using less energy and taking up less space in our ever-streamlined kitchens.

If there is one set back then it is an almost welcome one – oven gloves are a must again for handling sizzling hot combination baked delights!

What follows is my guide to the revolutionary combination microwave oven – how it works, how to time and cook items, the dishes and equipment you can use, how to cook whole meals, how to convert traditional favourites and tips for selecting the best cooking method. Complete with over some 100 recipes and basic cooking charts for everyday foods, all more than double-tested – I hope it will become your indispensable guide to combination microwave cooking.

CAROL BOWEN

Combination microwave cooking

Combination microwave cooking is a method of cooking
using microwave energy and conventional oven heat
simultaneously. But, as the name suggests, a combination
microwave cooker can cook by using only one cooking
method or by a mixture of several cooking methods –
sometimes up to as many as ten! Usually basic ovens have
a minimum of three cooking methods that they use:

Microwave only This facility can be used alone in exactly the
same way as you would use a basic microwave oven.

Convection only This mode of cooking is the same as that used
in a conventional oven but may be fan-assisted in some
cases. It is temperature controlled and is especially useful
for traditional cooking of some biscuits, batters, meringue
mixtures etc.

Combination This mode of cooking combines the microwave
system with the convection system to give fast cooking
results with traditional browning and crisping.

Grill only Some ovens offer a grill facility for traditional top
heat browning and crisping of items.

A mixture of other cooking methods include microwave with
grill; combination cooking with grill; fan-assisted grilling or
grilling with convection etc.
  Each manufacturer has his own method of producing
these systems within the combination microwave oven but
basically they fall into the following groups:

1 simultaneous convection with microwave power at a
   constant level;
2 simultaneous convection with pulsed or variable
   microwave power;
3 pulsed convection and microwave power.

1

Despite such variable systems and, one would imagine, their vastly different cooking performances, I have found, through lengthy testing, that results are very similar even though there is a wide variation of microwave output and convection settings. The chart on pages 12–13 will give you the equivalent settings to use on your oven in order to follow the recipes in this book and have been tested over a wide range of models to ensure success.

Types and features of combination ovens

Basically there are two types of combination microwave oven – the tabletop variety and the built-in type. Features can include touch control, push button or dial operation depending upon make. Operation usually involves selecting a convection temperature, microwave power level, cooking mode and time, although this differs from model to model. In some cases once the cooking mode has been selected the convection temperature and microwave level operate automatically on a preset level simply leaving you to decide upon the cooking time. In most cases where this pre-set or pre-programmed level is used, numbered or lettered guides help you to select the ideal one according to the food to be cooked. For example, setting 1 may be 160°C using 30% (low) microwave power and will prove ideal for cooking casseroles and hot pots. Your manufacturer's handbook will tell you exactly what the settings are on your oven and if it is pre-programmed to specific temperatures and power levels.

To follow the recipes in this book using an oven with *pre-set or pre-programmed* controls, select the setting that as near as possible resembles the temperature and power level recommended, erring on the side of safety with a slightly lower microwave power if not exact (remembering that it is better to slightly undercook, then add more time, rather than overcook). In every pre-programmed oven I tried I got excellent results from the recipes and the times only varied slightly from the original, and never by more than a few minutes.

Some manufacturers offer *two level cooking* by introducing a shelf into their ovens so that you can cook complete meals. A control will usually be incorporated to assist this type of cooking, ensuring that equal microwave energy and convection heat will reach both cooking levels – often a push button device.

Yet more variety comes with so-called *sensor cooking*, a feature often found on more expensive models. This method of combination cooking can be programmed to give excellent cooking results automatically – the oven automatically checks when the food is cooked by monitoring the moisture released into the oven cavity by the food during cooking.

One of the latest combination models boasts *halogen heat cooking* as an alternative to convection heat. Halogen heat filaments are set into windows in the roof and left-hand side of the oven to give top and side or all round browning. The oven can be used in several cooking modes with or without halogen heat: the oven will cook by microwave only; with top halogen heat only for a grill facility; with top and side halogen heat for convection style cooking without the microwave; with microwave and top halogen heat for combination cooking requiring top browning, e.g. gratins; and finally microwave with top and side halogen heat for all round browning and combination cooking of roasts, cakes, pastry items and so on.

A few ovens do have a special control for *preheating* the oven when necessary. Once selected this takes about five to ten minutes for operation and an audible reminder will usually indicate when the oven is ready to use. Many of the ovens I tested stated that no preheating was necessary. In some cases this proved to be correct but in others I was disappointed with browning performance. The best results almost invariably came from putting food into a hot oven that had been preheated (the only exceptions being long-cooked dishes like casseroles and large roasts). For this reason I have in many of the recipes that follow in the recipe section stated where preheating is necessary. If you find that your oven does brown sufficiently in recipes with times under thirty minutes then ignore the preheating advice. Fortunately preheating isn't the usual lengthy process we associate with conventional cooking – often it is as little as five minutes and usually no more than 12–15 minutes. For more information see page 11.

Advantages of combination cooking

Without doubt the microwave brought high technology into the kitchen and we all marvelled at the way in which it could cook, defrost and reheat foods in seconds and minutes rather than minutes and hours. Most of us manoeuvred round little problems like lack of browning and crisping since the time advantages were so startling. Imagine therefore a machine that could do everything a microwave could do and everything your conventional oven could do – married together! The advantages therefore speak for themselves – crisp brown food with all the traditional looks we love, cooked in a fraction of the time it takes to cook conventionally; speedily cooked food that loses very little nutritional value since cooking times are so precise and there is little risk of cooking away valuable vitamins and minerals; economical and efficient cooking using less energy since cooking times are shorter; and a bonus over the microwave alone, it will cook Yorkshire puddings, crisp pastries, meringues and other foods that are a disaster in a conventional microwave.

Basic combination oven accessories

The majority of tabletop combination microwave ovens have a *turntable* – usually made of ceramic or sometimes metal. It must be in position on the base of the oven for the oven to operate. Occasionally there is a provision for stopping the turntable from rotating during the convection only mode.
All ovens have a metal *wire rack* of some kind. In the larger built-in models this may simply be a straightforward oven rack (but instructions will be given as to its position in the oven, often on shelf level 2, for ideal combination cooking). In the tabletop models this is positioned on the turntable

4

and allows air to circulate round the food being cooked. That is not to say that you cannot cook food on the base of the oven without using the rack – indeed when two dishes are being cooked at the same time one may need to be placed on the turntable or base of the oven and the other on the wire rack above. Some models have as many as three racks – high, medium and low racks for combination cooking and combination grilling or grilling only. Always check your manufacturer's instructions for using the racks.

A *splash guard* is also supplied with some models – this is a perforated metal tray that fits on top of the turntable. It is principally used to stop splashing of cooking juices when the turntable is used as a drip tray. When an oven does not have a turntable then a glass drip tray is often supplied to fit into the base of the oven to catch cooking juices. Sometimes it may come with or will double up as a baking tray for cooking biscuits, pizzas and other flat baked items that require support. A handle may also be supplied with this for easy lifting out of the oven – useful since this does become hot.

Some manufacturers of ovens say that metal can be used in their ovens, others say not. Some go further and say some metal dishes can be introduced providing that they do not have metal lids. I have had mixed results with using metal tins (some extremely good and some terrible). Again it is important to check your manufacturer's advice. Some will provide a special *insulating mat* for this purpose – it should be placed between the metal tin and the wire rack or turntable during combination cooking to prevent arcing of the microwaves.

Cooking equipment and utensils

For microwave only

Never use metal cookware when using the microwave only mode of cooking. This includes metal bakeware, dishes with a metallic trim, cooking dishes with heavy cast-iron bases, lead crystal, plates and cups with a metallic trim or signature on the base and metal convenience style throw-away dishes. Melamine isn't suitable since it tends to char and non-dishwasher-proof plastics tend to distort.

For best results use glass, glazed ceramic, dishwasher-proof plastics, special microwave cookware, china, pottery, roasting bags and cook bags and, for short cooking times, wood, wicker, paper, linen or cotton napkins and greaseproof paper.

For convection only

All the dishes that one usually associates with conventional cooking can be used here – ovenproof glass, ovenproof ceramics, metal baking tins and trays, cast-iron dishes and casseroles, ovenproof plastics (although check their temperature ceiling) and earthenware. Do not use plastics, lead crystal and cling film. Oven gloves are a must.

For combination baking

Always check here what your manufacturer recommends. Some allow the use of metals, some do not. All models will find the following cookware suitable for use (and these are the principle dishes used in the recipes that follow): ovenproof glass, ovenproof ceramics, roasting bags and occasionally some special heat-resistant plastics (again only up to certain temperatures). Perhaps the best investment is a good range of freezer to ovenproof glass. This can be used in all three types of cooking and can also be taken from freezer to combination microwave oven without fear of shattering. Manufacturer's today recognize the growing role of the microwave and have steadily expanded their range of such glass to produce traditional metal bakeware shapes in this material for excellent cooking results.

Since dishes will get hot with this mode of cooking it is important to remember to wear oven gloves for handling dishes.

Cleaning and care of your combination microwave oven

It is important to wipe any splatters or spills from the interior of the oven after cooking – use a soft damp cloth or sponge, using a non-scratch cream cleanser if necessary. This prevents the build-up of baked-on food and is best done when the oven cavity is warm (but not hot). If there is a wave guide in the ceiling of the oven then wipe this with a soft damp cloth to remove any food debris that may have collected there. Clean the outside of the oven with mild soap and water and rinse dry with a soft cloth – it shouldn't be necessary to use any abrasive cleaner. Always try to avoid letting the controls or control panel become soiled by regularly cleaning. When cleaning this always open the door of the oven to inactivate the control panel.

As with all microwave ovens check the seal round the door to make sure it has not become dirty and will not form a good seal when closed. Remove the turntable and wire racks to clean in warm soapy water.

If you have a halogen heat model then do not attempt to clean the halogen lamps until the glass lamp covers are completely cool. Use a non-scratch cream cleanser with a scotch brite then wipe with a clean damp cloth.

Never tamper with the inside controls of a combination microwave oven – call in a qualified engineer. Consider, too, a regular annual service check and comprehensive insurance if your machine is out of warranty.

Selecting the best cooking method

You can literally have the best of three or more worlds with the combination microwave oven – use the different cooking modes to their best effect by selecting the ideal one for the food to be cooked.

Microwave only This is ideal for making speedy soups that do not require a crisp or brown finish; cooking fresh and frozen vegetables; cooking fresh and frozen fruits; cooking rice, pasta, grains and pulses; making steamed puddings where browning and crisping are not important; whizzing up a speedy, smooth and silky sauce to serve with a roast, vegetable or pudding; and cooking eggs in all their guises from scrambled to baked (although not boiled).

Convection only Use the convection cooking mode for baking small cakes, soufflés, cooking choux pastries and biscuits where the circulated hot air will give the browning, crisping and overall cooking performance you require in a controlled time. The addition of the microwave in cooking these items is not usually very beneficial since the quicker cooking times they would promote may mean that the dishes do not brown so efficiently, will not rise to the expected heights and may not crisp sufficiently.

Combination baking This mode of cooking reaps all the benefits of microwave and convection cooking. It is ideal for cooking small and large cuts of meat, poultry and game; cooking pieces of, or whole, fish; cooking vegetable gratins; baking puff and shortcrust pastry pies of all kinds; cooking sweet and savoury pastries large and small; making quiches, flans and tarts; baking sweet puddings, cakes, breads and teabreads; and making whole meals in a fraction of the time it would normally take.

Combination grilling If your oven has this facility then it may be preferable to cook small cuts of meat, poultry, game and fish on this mode along with kebabs, bacon and sausages. Some convenience style grillable items can also be cooked this way.

Converting favourite recipes

Wherever possible look for a recipe in this book or in your combination microwave handbook and use it as a guide to cooking your own favourite recipe. Undoubtedly you will find at least some components of the recipe that are duplicated elsewhere, whether it be making a sauce to bind ingredients together; baking a pie with a similar pie crust and raw, cooked or par-cooked filling; making a similar style teabread or cake, for example, that will give you some close indication of what power level, convection setting or combination bake mode to use. Always err on the side of safety and undertime rather than overtime for good results and make a note of any times and changes you perhaps would like to make when cooking the recipe again.

As a general rule choose a higher temperature than normally used conventionally and a 30% (low) power microwave level

I always feel like hiding behind my hands when I say rely upon your own judgement and knowledge of your own particular model – it seems like I'm opting out of giving hard and fast rules. The truth is that even two models of the same microwave model will still perform differently (just like two cars of the same make will have a slightly different performance, may break down at different times and may give years of good – or bad – service). Getting to know your microwave, living with it and perhaps learning to love it are the best tips I can give for getting the best out of it beyond the handbook and recipe book.

However, in general, do not use the combination oven to cook favourite recipes with high rise batters – use the convection only mode. Use convection only too for small cakes, individual tarts, meringues, small sponges, biscuits and individual scones. Other sweet baked items are better suited to combination baking. These include gingerbreads, madeira cakes and all those teabreads that generally are a denser type of cake and normally cook at a lower temperature over a long period of time. The combination mode is excellent for cooking pastries both small and large like vol-au-vents, jalousies, plaits, turnovers and mille-feuilles. Bread in loaves, rolls or shaped rounds also cook extremely well.

Leave the microwave only mode to cope with vegetable

9

and fruit dishes unless they have a crisp crumble type topping or gratin style finish. Pasta and rice are also better cooked in the microwave or on the conventional hob. If the microwave is free then it will cook these items in about the same length of time as conventionally but there is less risk of sticking and no baked-on pan to cope with afterwards. If the microwave is in use making a sauce or filling for the same then turn back to the hob for assistance. Remember the microwave is supposed to be an aid to the well run kitchen; don't be afraid to mix and match it with your other cooking appliances to best effect – it needn't do everything at the expense of time and effort.

Before you start . . . recipe guidelines

It is strongly recommended that you read the introductory section to this book for good results with microwave combination cooking

- All the recipes and timings in this book have been tested using a variety of microwave combination ovens. The timings and instructions given in the recipes that follow assume that the microwave only mode of cooking has variable power and the descriptions used refer to the following power outputs:

  100% (high) = 600 watts
  50% (medium) = 300 watts
  30% (low) = 180 watts

  These power levels have been used with a range of convection cooking temperatures from 160°C to 450°C. If your oven has different power level settings or pre-set levels of combination cooking then refer to the chart overleaf – it covers all existing microwave combination ovens and will guide you as to which microwave level to use.
- It has been assumed in the recipes that a turntable facility is in use – recipe instructions therefore give the best cookware to use for this and instructions for two-tier

10

cooking using the wire rack. If your oven does not have a turntable then a larger dish can often be used and cooking may be able to take place simply on one level.

- It has also been assumed that metal cannot be used in the oven and all instructions for cookware reflect this. If your manufacturer states that metal can be used and you find good results then opt for this kind of bakeware if liked.

- Metric measurements may vary from one recipe to another within the book for best results. It is essential to follow only one set of measures, either metric or imperial.

- Since preheating was found to be necessary for some ovens all the recipes that benefit from preheating have been given those instructions. If your oven works well without preheating then ignore. If a recipe does not include any preheating instructions then it is unnecessary for good brown results.

- Note that unless otherwise stated, flour is of the plain variety, water is cold, eggs are size 3, sugar is granulated and all spoon quantities are measured level.

- Standing times are generally not as important in combination microwave cooking as microwave only cooking. However, do allow a standing time of about ten minutes when cooking large roasts – they are easier to carve after resting. The same is true of cakes and teabreads – leave to stand in the dish for five minutes to rest before turning out on to a wire rack to cool.

- When using the combination bake mode do not cover dishes unless otherwise stated, for this can affect the browning of foods. Never use foil or cling film for this purpose.

- Stir and turn foods according to the specific recipe instructions.

- Government guidelines now recommend that cling film with plasticizers, i.e. pvc film, should not be used as a covering or lining for foods cooked in the microwave. All cling film referred to in this book is of the 'polyethylene' film type without plasticizers and can be found under such brand names as Purecling, Saran Wrap and Glad

Guide to comparative combination microwave oven controls

	100% (high)	50% (medium)	30% (low)	Grilling facility
Description of settings used in this book (with 140°–250°C)				yes
Descriptions of settings available on other popular combination microwave ovens:				
BEJAM BM801	high speed+	high speed	high speed−	no
BELLING TRIPLETTE 343	high	medium	low	no
BOSCH HMG 2000	600	180+	180	yes
HMG 2200	600	180+	180	yes
HMG 2010	4	3	2	yes
HMG 2210	4	3	2	yes
MULTIMICRO HBE 6920	1	2	3	yes
HBE 6900	1	2	3	yes
CREDA MICROWAVE CIRCULAIRE	high	low/roast	defrost	yes
FAGOR MW 2100 UK	full	medium+	medium	yes
GAGGENAU (to be launched in 1988)	100%	50%	25%+	yes
BROTHER 2000	high	medium	low	no
2100	high speed+	high speed	high speed−	
MF2200	high speed+	high speed	high speed−	
HOTPOINT 6680	600	180+	180	yes

MIELE	N700 (to be launched in 1988)	600	300	150	—
NEFF	6180	600	180+	180	yes'
	6185	600	180+	180	yes
PANASONIC	NE993/992	2+	2	3	yes
	NE972	2+	2	3	yes
SCHOLTES	F2860	5	$^2/_3$	$^1/_2$	yes
	F2865	5	$^2/_3$	$^1/_2$	yes
SHARP	8170	100%	50%	30%	no
	8270	100%	50%	30%	no
	8560	100%	50%	30%	no
SIEMENS	HF4200	600	180+	180	yes
	HF4202	600	180+	180	yes
	HF6504	4	3	1	yes
	HF6502	4	3	1	yes
	HB8704	1	2	3	yes
THORN MULTIWAVE WITH HALOGEN HEAT					
	MH1080	full	medium	defrost	yes
TOSHIBA	ER9610	high	medium low/medium	medium low/low	no

Note: + This is the equivalent setting to use but increase times slightly.

  − This is the equivalent setting to use but decrease times slightly.

Wrap. This type of film does not cling as well as standard pvc film but can often be more manageable when pulling back to stir foods during microwave cooking. If you do not wish to use cling film as a covering then use an upturned plate, saucer, special microwave plate cover or baking parchment instead.

What went wrong?

Excessive splattering of juices and smoking fats

- Reduce the microwave power level, convection temperature setting or both next time and increase the time slightly.
- Remove excess cooking fats halfway during the cooking time with a bulb baster, or pour off.

Poor browning of baked items

- Increase the convection temperature next time.
- If possible cook by convection only for five to ten minutes at the end of the cooking time – if surface browning is sufficient use the grill only for this purpose.
- Preheat the oven before cooking the food.

Undercooked food with adequate browning

- Increase the microwave power level.
- Decrease the convection temperature and cook for a little longer.

Base of pastry items raw and undercooked

- Pre-cook the pastry base if possible before adding filling (200°C at 30% microwave power in a preheated oven is usually sufficient).
- Use a heated metal try (if allowed) or the baking tray or sheet provided with the oven to stand the dish or raw pastry item on – this will effectively crisp the base and help conduct heat into the pastry.

14

Food generally not brown and crisp enough

- Preheat the oven next time cooking this recipe.
- Increase the convection temperature in 10°C stages until desired result is achieved.
- Use convection only or grill only for the last few minutes of the cooking until desired degree of browning and crisping is achieved without risking overcooking.

Food dried out

- Add a little more water or liquid next time (combination microwave cookery does seem to require marginally more liquid than microwave cooking alone for the same style dish).

Remember to make a note of all your changes for successful results next time

Recipes

Soups and starters

Brandied French onion soup with Swiss cheese floats

Microwave only: 100% (high)
Combination bake: 250°C using 50% (medium)
Serves: 4
Total cooking time: 18–20 minutes

25g/1oz butter
675g/1½lb onions, peeled and finely sliced
1 tbsp flour
1.2 litres/2 pints hot rich beef stock
salt and pepper
4 tbsp brandy
4 slices French bread
50g/2oz Gruyère cheese, grated

Place the butter and onions in a large ovenproof soup tureen or casserole dish. Cover and microwave at 100% (high) microwave only for 5 minutes, stirring once. Stir in the flour, blending well. Add the stock and salt and pepper to taste, blending well. Cover and microwave at 100% (high) microwave only for 10 minutes, stirring once, or until the soup is boiling and thickened and the onions are cooked. Remove from the oven and stir in the brandy.

Preheat the oven to 250°C.

Sprinkle the slices of French bread with the cheese and float on top of the soup. Combination bake at 250°C using 50% (medium) microwave power for 3–5 minutes, or until the cheese has melted, is bubbling and light brown. Serve at once.

Cheesy niblets soufflé

Microwave only: 100% (high)
Combination bake: 250°C using 50% (medium)
Serves: 4
Total cooking time: 16 minutes

50g/2oz butter or margarine
50g/2oz plain flour

300ml/½ pint milk
100g/4oz mature Cheddar cheese, grated
pinch of dry mustard powder
3 eggs, separated
198g/7oz can sweetcorn kernels, drained
salt and pepper

Place the butter or margarine in a bowl and microwave at
100% (high) microwave only for 1 minute to melt. Stir in
the flour, then gradually add the milk. Microwave at 100%
(high) microwave only for 3 minutes, stirring every 1
minute, until smooth, boiling and thickened. Stir in the
cheese, mustard and egg yolks, blending well.

Whisk the egg whites until they stand in stiff peaks. Fold
into the sauce with the sweetcorn and salt and pepper to
taste. Pour into a greased 1.5 litre/2½ pint soufflé dish.
Place on the wire rack and combination bake at 250°C
using 50% (medium) microwave power for 12 minutes, or
until well risen, golden and cooked. Serve at once.

Baked crab-stuffed avocados

Combination bake: 250°C using 50% (medium)
Serves: 4
Total cooking time: 5 minutes

2 large ripe avocados
lemon juice
225g/8oz fresh crabmeat or 200g/7oz can crab, drained
4 tbsp mayonnaise
2 tsp snipped chives
½ clove garlic, crushed (optional)
2 spring onions, finely chopped
1 tbsp red wine vinegar
1 egg white
lemon twists to garnish

Preheat the oven to 250°C. Halve the avocados and remove
the stones. Sprinkle with lemon juice to prevent the flesh
from turning brown. Mix the crabmeat with the mayonnaise,
chives, garlic if used, spring onions and red wine vinegar.
Whisk the egg white until it stands in stiff peaks and fold

into the crab mixture, blending well. Spoon into the
avocado hollows.

Place in ovenproof avocado dishes or a large flan dish and
secure in position with crumpled greaseproof paper.
Combination bake at once at 250°C using 50% (medium)
microwave power for 5 minutes or until the filling has set,
is puffed and golden brown. Serve at once garnished with
lemon twists.

Barbecued spareribs

Combination bake: 200°C using 30% (low)
Serves: 4
Total cooking time: 35 minutes

3 tbsp tomato ketchup
3 tbsp tomato chilli relish
2 tbsp Worcestershire sauce
dash of chilli sauce
2 tbsp red wine vinegar
2 tbsp brown sugar
4 tbsp soy sauce
2 tsp mild burger mustard
½ onion, peeled and grated
salt and pepper
1kg/2lb pork spareribs, cut into ribs

Mix the tomato ketchup with the tomato chilli relish,
Worcestershire sauce, chilli sauce, vinegar, sugar, soy
sauce, mustard, onion and salt and pepper to taste, blending
well.

Place the spareribs in a shallow baking dish and pour
over the barbecue sauce. Combination bake at 200°C using
30% (low) microwave power for 35 minutes, turning over
twice. Serve hot as a delicious starter. Serve these sticky
ribs with napkins.

Eggs en cocotte

Microwave only: 100% (high)
Combination bake: 250°C using 50% (medium)

Serves: 4
Total cooking time: 12–14 minutes

15g/½oz butter
1 bunch spring onions, trimmed and chopped
100g/4oz mushrooms, wiped and sliced
100g/4oz tub Castello Bouquet soft cheese with garlic and herbs
salt and pepper
4 eggs
4 tbsp single cream
snipped chives to garnish

Place the butter, spring onions and mushrooms in a bowl. Cover and microwave at 100% (high) microwave only for 4 minutes, stirring twice, until soft. Add the cheese and salt and pepper to taste and stir until the cheese has melted.

Divide the mixture between four greased ramekin dishes. Make a well in the centre of each and crack an egg into it. Season with salt and pepper to taste and spoon the cream equally over the eggs.

Combination bake at 250°C using 50% (medium) microwave power for 8–10 minutes or until the whites are just set but the yolks are still soft. Garnish with snipped chives and serve at once with toast or crusty bread.

Duck pâté en croûte

Microwave only: 100% (high)
Combination bake: 220°C using 30% (low)
Serves: 6
Total cooking time: 20½–22½ minutes

Pastry:
20g/¾oz lard
125ml/4fl oz milk
175g/6oz plain flour
beaten egg to glaze
Filling:
100g/4oz chicken livers, trimmed and finely chopped
225g/8oz duck, boned and minced
225g/8oz pork fillet, minced
1 small onion, peeled and finely chopped

1 garlic clove, peeled and crushed
½ tsp mixed dried herbs
pinch of ground mixed spice
grated rind of ½ orange
1 tbsp brandy
salt and pepper

Line a 450g/1lb loaf dish with greaseproof paper or cling film, leaving the paper high enough at the sides so that the pâté can be lifted out of the dish later.

To make the pastry, place the lard and milk in a bowl and microwave at 100% (high) microwave only for 2½ minutes. Add the flour and beat to a smooth dough. When cool enough to handle, knead lightly to make a smooth dough. Divide the pastry into two-thirds and one-third portions. Place the larger piece in the prepared loaf dish and using the fingers mould on to the base and up the sides of the dish.

Mix the chicken livers with the duck, pork, onion, garlic, herbs, spice, orange rind, brandy and salt and pepper to taste, blending well. Pack into the pastry-lined dish, pressing down well. Brush around the rim of the dish with beaten egg.

Roll out the remaining pastry to make a lid and place in position. Trim, seal and flute the edges. Make a small hole in the centre of the pie to allow any steam to escape. Decorate with any pastry trimmings and glaze with beaten egg. Carefully lift the pâté from the dish with the cling film or greaseproof paper and place on a flan dish, removing the paper or film. Glaze the sides with beaten egg.

Preheat the oven to 220°C.

Combination bake at 220°C using 30% (low) microwave power for 18–20 minutes. Allow to cool. Serve cut in slices.

Variation:

Bosch pâté en croûte with Cumberland sauce

Prepare and cook as above but use 100g/4oz chopped lamb's liver mixed with 225g/8oz sausagemeat, 225g/8oz minced lean pork, 1 finely chopped onion, 1 crushed clove garlic, ½ tsp dried sage, 1 tbsp sherry and salt and pepper to taste for the filling. Serve with a Cumberland sauce made by placing the pared rind of 1 orange and lemon, cut into julienne strips, in a bowl with 2 tbsp water. Cover and microwave at 100% (high) microwave only for 2 minutes. Drain. Add 4 tbsp redcurrant jelly, 4 tbsp port, ½ tsp mustard powder, ½ tsp ground ginger and the juice from the orange and lemon, blending well. Microwave at 100% (high) microwave only for 3 minutes, stirring once. Blend 1 tsp arrowroot powder with 1 tbsp water and stir into the sauce. Microwave at 100% (high) microwave only for a further 1 minute, stirring twice. Leave to cool then serve with the pâté.

Quick meals, snacks and suppers

Apple and bacon koulibiac

Microwave only: 100% (high) and 50% (medium)
Combination bake: 250°C using 50% (medium)
Serves: 6
Total cooking time: 23–25 minutes

75g/3oz long-grain rice
300ml/½ pint boiling water
1 leek, trimmed and finely sliced
1 large Bramley apple peeled, cored and chopped
2 tbsp chopped parsley
2 hard-boiled eggs, shelled and chopped
225g/8oz cooked bacon or ham, chopped
25g/1oz butter
salt and pepper
370g/13oz packet frozen puff pastry, thawed
beaten egg to glaze

Place the rice, water and leek in a bowl, cover and
microwave at 100% (high) microwave only for 3 minutes.
Reduce the power setting to 50% (medium) microwave only
and cook for a further 12 minutes, stirring once. Leave to
stand for 3 minutes then add the apple, parsley, eggs, bacon
or ham, butter and salt and pepper to taste, blending well.

Preheat the oven to 250°C.

Cut the puff pastry in half and roll out each half, on a
lightly floured surface, to an oval shape measuring about
18 × 25cm/7 × 10in. Pile the filling mixture into the centre
of one of the pastry slices, pressing together well to mound
to a neat pile. Brush the edges of the pastry with beaten egg
then cover with the second pastry slice. Pinch the edges of
the pastries together to secure and crimp decoratively. Place
on a large ovenproof glass quiche or flan dish and glaze
with beaten egg. If liked, pastry leaves can be made from
the trimmings and placed on top of the koulibiac then glaze
again with beaten egg. Make small slits in the surface of the
koulibiac with scissors or a sharp knife and combination
bake at 250°C using 50% (medium) microwave power for
8–10 minutes, or until well risen, cooked and golden brown.

Serve hot or cold with seasonal vegetables or salad and a
yogurt or soured cream dressing. A delicious picnic recipe.

Smoked haddock soufflé

Microwave only: 100% (high)
Combination bake: 250°C using 50% (medium)
Serves: 4
Total cooking time: 16 minutes

2 tbsp grated Parmesan cheese
50g/2oz butter or margarine
50g/2oz plain flour
300ml/½ pint milk
50g/2oz grated cheese
3 eggs, separated
225g/8oz cooked smoked haddock, skinned, boned and flaked
salt and pepper

Lightly grease a 1.5 litre/2½ pint soufflé dish and sprinkle the base and sides with the Parmesan cheese.

Place the butter or margarine in a bowl and microwave at 100% (high) microwave only for 1 minute to melt. Stir in the flour then gradually add the milk. Microwave at 100% (high) microwave only for 3 minutes, stirring every 1 minute, until smooth, boiling and thickened. Stir in the cheese and egg yolks, blending well.

Whisk the egg whites until they stand in stiff peaks. Fold into the sauce with the haddock and salt and pepper to taste. Pour into the prepared dish. Place on the wire rack and combination bake at 250°C using 50% (medium) microwave power for 12 minutes, or until well risen, golden and cooked. Serve at once.

Cauliflower and pasta bake

Microwave only: 100% (high)
Combination bake: 250°C using 50% (medium)
Serves: 4
Total cooking time: 21–22 minutes

450g/1lb cauliflower florets
2 tbsp water
25g/1oz butter
25g/1oz plain flour

300ml/½ pint milk
100g/4oz Cheddar cheese, grated
salt and pepper
175g/6oz cooked pasta shapes
6 rashers cooked streaky or back bacon, crumbled

Place the cauliflower and water in a medium sized casserole
dish. Cover and microwave at 100% (high) microwave
only for 10 minutes, stirring once. Remove and drain
thoroughly.

Place the butter in a jug and microwave at 100% (high)
microwave only for 1 minute to melt. Blend in the flour
and milk. Microwave at 100% (high) microwave only for 3
minutes, stirring every 1 minute, until boiling, smooth and
thickened. Stir in half of the cheese, blending well.

Mix the cauliflower with the cooked pasta, half of the
bacon and the cheese sauce, blending well. Sprinkle with
the remaining cheese and bacon. Combination bake at 250°C
using 50% (medium) microwave power for 7–8 minutes,
or until golden, cooked and bubbly. Serve at once.

Haddock and sweetcorn quiche

Microwave only: 100% (high)
Combination bake: 200°C using 30% (low)
Serves: 6
Total cooking time: 23–29 minutes

Pastry:
175g/6oz wheatmeal flour
40g/1½oz butter or margarine
40g/1½oz lard
2–3 tbsp cold water
Filling:
225g/8oz smoked haddock
2 tbsp milk
198g/7oz can sweetcorn kernels, drained
150ml/¼ pint natural yogurt
2 eggs, beaten
1 tbsp chopped parsley
salt and pepper

Topping:
50g/2oz wholemeal breadcrumbs
25g/1oz grated cheese
½ tsp curry powder

To make the pastry, sift the flour into a bowl, adding the bran left in the sieve. Rub in the butter or margarine and lard until the mixture resembles fine breadcrumbs. Stir in the water and bind to a firm but pliable dough. Knead lightly on a lightly floured surface then roll out to a round large enough to line the base and sides of a 20cm/8in flan dish. Prick the base with a fork.

Place the haddock in a dish with the milk. Cover and microwave at 100% (high) microwave only for 3–4 minutes, until cooked. Drain the milk from the fish and reserve. Skin, bone and flake the fish.

Preheat the oven to 200°C.

Place the fish and sweetcorn in the base of the flan. Mix the yogurt with the reserved milk, eggs, parsley and salt and pepper to taste, blending well. Pour over the fish mixture. Mix all the topping ingredients together and sprinkle over the flan.

Combination bake at 200°C using 30% (low) microwave power for 20–25 minutes, until golden, crisp and firm to the touch. Serve hot or cold, cut into wedges.

Cheesy bacon quiche

Microwave only: 100% (high)
Combination bake: 200°C using 30% (low)
Serves: 6
Total cooking time: 23½–24 minutes

Pastry:
175g/6oz plain or wheatmeal flour
pinch of salt
75g/3oz butter or margarine
2–3 tbsp cold water
Filling:
15g/½oz butter
1 onion, peeled and finely chopped

100g/4oz bacon, rinded and chopped
100g/4oz grated cheese
2 eggs, beaten
milk
salt and pepper
2 tomatoes, sliced

To make the pastry, sift the flour into a bowl, adding any
bran left in the sieve if using wheatmeal flour. Rub in the
butter or margarine until the mixture resembles fine
breadcrumbs. Stir in the water and bind to a firm but
pliable dough. Knead lightly on a lightly floured surface
then roll out to a round large enough to line the base and
sides of a 20cm/8in flan dish. Prick the base with a fork.

Place the butter, onion and bacon in a dish and microwave
at 100% (high) microwave only for 3½–4 minutes, stirring
once, until cooked. Allow to cool slightly then place in the
base of the flan.

Preheat the oven to 200°C.

Sprinkle the cheese over the bacon mixture. Mix the eggs
with sufficient milk to make up to 300ml/½ pint. Season
to taste with salt and pepper and pour over the cheese and
bacon layers. Carefully top with the sliced tomatoes.

Combination bake at 200°C using 30% (low) microwave
power for 20 minutes, or until firm to the touch, golden
brown and the pastry is crisp. Serve hot or cold, cut into
wedges, with a seasonal crisp salad.

Speedy four seasons pizza

Combination bake: 210°C using 30% (low)
Serves: 4
Total cooking time: 15–20 minutes

Pizza base:
225g/8oz self-raising flour
1 tsp baking powder
50g/2oz butter or margarine
150ml/¼ pint milk or milk and water mixed
Toppings:
3 tbsp tomato purée

1 tomato, peeled and chopped
½ onion, peeled and finely chopped
2 tsp mild burger mustard
1 tsp dried basil
salt and pepper
50g/2oz cooked ham, chopped
50g/2oz mushrooms, wiped and sliced
4 slices salami, rinded
75g/3oz frozen stir-fry vegetables, thawed
3 sardines or 50g/2oz peeled prawns
225g/8oz Cheddar cheese, grated or Mozarella cheese, thinly sliced

To make the base, sift the flour with the baking powder.
Rub in the butter until the mixture resembles fine
breadcrumbs. Stir in the milk and bind to a firm dough.
Knead lightly then roll out, on a lightly floured surface, to
a large round (checking the size of your oven) or 4 small
individual rounds – about 15cm/6in wide. Place on a
greased baking tray or large ovenproof plate.

Mix the tomato purée with the onion, tomato, burger
mustard, basil and salt and pepper to taste, blending well.
Spread over the pizza base. Top each quarter of the pizza
or each individual pizza with the ham mixed with the
mushrooms, the salami, the vegetables and sardines or
prawns. Sprinkle with the grated cheese.

Combination bake at 210°C using 30% (low) microwave
power for 15–20 minutes or until cooked, golden and
bubbly. Serve hot with a crisp green salad.

Bacon hotpot with dumplings

Microwave only: 100% (high)
Combination bake: 200°C using 30% (low)
Serves: 4–5
Total cooking time: 47 minutes

25g/1oz butter
2 onions, peeled and sliced
3 carrots, peeled and sliced
425g/15oz can tomatoes
675g/1½lb cooked forehock or collar bacon, cubed

1 tsp dried mixed herbs
300ml/½ pint boiling vegetable stock
salt and pepper
Dumplings:
175g/6oz self-raising flour
75g/3oz shredded beef suet
1 tsp salt
cold water to mix

Place the butter and onions in a casserole dish and microwave at 100% (high) microwave only for 3 minutes, stirring once. Add the carrots and microwave at 100% (high) microwave only for a further 4 minutes, stirring once. Add the tomatoes, bacon, herbs, stock and salt and pepper to taste, blending well. Cover and combination bake at 200°C using 30% (low) for 20 minutes.

Meanwhile to make the dumplings, mix the flour with the suet and salt. Stir in enough cold water to make a stiff dough. Divide and shape into 8 small balls and add to the casserole, basting well with the stock. Cover and combination bake at 200°C using 30% (low) for 10 minutes. Remove the lid and cook by convection only at 200°C for a further 10 minutes. Serve hot straight from the dish.

Sunset shepherd's pie

Microwave only: 100% (high)
Combination bake: 200°C using 50% (medium)
Serves: 4
Total cooking time: 43–46 minutes

675g/1½lb potatoes, peeled and sliced
8 tbsp water
25g/1oz butter
1–2 tbsp milk
salt and pepper
350g/12oz minced beef or raw minced lamb
1 onion, peeled and chopped
100g/4oz mixed diced frozen vegetables, thawed
2 tomatoes, peeled and sliced
50g/2oz mushrooms, wiped and sliced
4 tbsp beef stock

1 tbsp tomato ketchup or purée
50g/2oz grated cheese to sprinkle

Place the potatoes and water in a bowl. Cover and
microwave at 100% (high) microwave only for 12 minutes,
stirring once, until tender. Drain and mash with the butter,
milk and salt and pepper to taste until smooth and fluffy.

Place the meat in a dish and microwave at 100% (high)
microwave only for 5 minutes, stirring twice to break up
any lumps. Remove the meat with a slotted spoon and add
the onion and vegetables to the dish juices. Cover and
microwave at 100% (high) microwave only for 4 minutes.
Add the meat, tomatoes, mushrooms and salt and pepper
to taste, blending well. Spoon into a deep ovenproof dish
and pour over the stock mixed with the tomato ketchup or
purée. Pipe or spoon the potato over the top and sprinkle
with the grated cheese.

Combination bake at 200°C using 50% (medium)
microwave power for 22–25 minutes or until crisp and
golden. Serve hot.

Cheese and chive soufflette

Microwave only: 100% (high)
Combination bake: 250°C using 100% (high)
Serves: 4
Total cooking time: 11 minutes

few dry breadcrumbs
25g/1oz butter
25g/1oz plain flour
200ml/7fl oz milk
100g/4oz Double Gloucester cheese, grated
1 tbsp chive mustard
¼ tsp ground nutmeg
salt and pepper
4 eggs, separated

Butter a 1.2 litre/2 pint soufflé dish and coat the inside
lightly with dry breadcrumbs.

Place the butter in a jug and microwave at 100% (high)
microwave only for 1 minute. Stir in the flour then blend

in the milk. Microwave at 100% (high) microwave only for 3 minutes, stirring every 1 minute, until boiling, smooth and thickened.

Preheat the oven to 250°C.

Stir the cheese into the sauce with the mustard, nutmeg and salt and pepper to taste. Stir in the egg yolks, blending well.

Whisk the egg whites until they stand in stiff peaks. Fold into the sauce mixture with a metal spoon. Pour into the prepared soufflé dish and combination bake at 250°C using 100% (high) for 7 minutes or until well risen, golden and just firm when lightly shaken. Serve at once.

Combination baking guide for convenience foods

Item	Temperature	Microwave power level	Total cooking time in minutes
425g/15oz shepherd's pie	220°C	medium	10–12
400g/14oz fish pie	220°C	medium	10–12
425g/15oz moussaka	220°C	medium	9–11
400g/14oz cauliflower cheese	220°C	medium	9–11
275g/10oz vegetables au gratin	220°C	high	8–9
325g/11oz chicken in sauce with pasta	220°C	high	7
275g/10oz sausage and mash	220°C	high	7
280g/10oz fish fillet au gratin	220°C	high	9

Note: Times are from defrosted state. If items are frozen then thaw using microwave only.

Combination baking guide for 1 portion convenience meals

Meal	Temperature	Microwave power level	Total cooking time in minutes
1 portion frozen oven chips and frozen portion fish in breadcrumbs	250°C	medium	8
4 frozen fish fingers, 1 portion frozen oven chips and portion baked beans	250°C	medium	10–11
1 pork chop, little sliced apple, portion frozen green beans, pricked whole tomato	250°C	medium	13
1 pricked sausage, rasher of back bacon, portion of baked beans, pierced egg in dish	250°C	medium	6
1 pricked jacket potato, 175g/6oz steak, sliced onions and sliced mushrooms	250°C	medium	13

Mid-week and family main meals

Mariner's parcels

Combination bake: 250°C using 50% (medium)
Serves: 4
Total cooking time: 12–15 minutes

370g/13oz packet frozen puff pastry. thawed
100g/4oz Danish mycella cheese. crumbled
99g/3½oz can salmon, drained, bones removed and flaked
50g/2oz frozen mixed vegetables, thawed
25g/1oz fresh white breadcrumbs
pepper
1 egg, beaten

Roll out the pastry, on a lightly floured surface, and use to make four 13cm/5in squares, with trimmings for decorating the parcels.

Preheat the oven to 250°C.

Mix the cheese with the salmon, vegetables, breadcrumbs, pepper to taste and about one-third of the beaten egg, blending well.

Brush the edges of the pastry pieces with beaten egg and mound an equal quantity of the filling in the centre. Secure into parcels by bringing each corner of pastry into the centre and pinching together securely to enclose the filling.

Make decorative pastry leaves or fish shapes from the trimmings and secure to the parcels with beaten egg. Place on a large greased plate or flan dish and glaze with beaten egg.

Combination bake at 250°C using 50% (medium) microwave power for 12–15 minutes, or until the pastry is well risen and golden brown. Serve hot or cold.

Variation

If liked the salmon in the above recipe may be changed for tuna fish or chopped ham.

Haddock, celeriac and Roquefort fish pie

Microwave only: 100% (high)
Combination bake: 220°C using 50% (medium)
Serves: 4
Total cooking time: 20 minutes

225g/8oz peeled celeriac, cut into thin julienne strips
2 tbsp water
2 tsp lemon juice
25g/1oz butter
1 onion, peeled and chopped
25g/1oz plain flour
300ml/½ pint milk
50g/2oz Roquefort cheese, crumbled
½ bunch watercress, trimmed and chopped
salt and pepper
350g/12oz haddock fillet, skinned and cut into bite-sized pieces
250g/8¾oz packet frozen puff pastry, thawed
beaten egg to glaze

Place the celeriac in a bowl with the water. Cover and microwave at 100% (high) microwave only for 4 minutes, stirring once. Drain and toss in the lemon juice.

Place the butter in a bowl with the onion, cover and microwave at 100% (high) microwave only for 3 minutes, stirring once. Add the flour, blending well then gradually add the milk. Microwave at 100% (high) microwave only for a further 3 minutes, stirring every 1 minute until smooth, boiling and thickened. Add the Roquefort cheese, watercress and salt and pepper to taste, blending well. Fold in the haddock fillet and celeriac.

Preheat the oven to 220°C.

Spoon the fish mixture into a medium pie dish. Roll out the pastry, on a lightly floured surface, to an oval or round about 4cm/1½in larger than the pie dish. Trim a 2.5cm/1in strip from the edge of the pastry to make a pastry collar. Moisten the pie dish rim with water and press the pastry collar firmly on to the rim, overlapping the ends. Dampen the pastry collar with water then top with the pastry lid and press firmly together. Trim away any excess pastry with a knife and knock up the crust to seal. Flute the edges of the pie and decorate with any pastry trimmings if liked. Glaze with beaten egg and combination bake at 220°C using 50% (medium) microwave power for 10 minutes, or until the pastry is well risen, cooked and golden brown.

Serve hot with seasonal vegetables or a crisp salad.

Trout in creamy mushroom and celery sauce

Microwave only: 100% (high)
Combination bake: 230°C using 30% (low)
Serves: 4
Total cooking time: 15 minutes

1 tbsp oil
3 sticks celery, scrubbed and finely chopped
225g/8oz closed cup mushrooms, wiped and sliced
3 tbsp chopped parsley
grated rind of 1 large lemon
2 tsp cornflour
150ml/¼ pint soured cream
salt and pepper
4 trout, gutted and cleaned
1 tbsp fresh white breadcrumbs

Place the oil and celery in a bowl. Cover and microwave at 100% (high) microwave only for 2 minutes. Add the mushrooms, blending well. Cover and microwave at 100% (high) microwave only for 3 minutes, stirring once. Add the parsley, lemon rind and cornflour, blending well. Add the soured cream and salt and pepper to taste, blending well.

Preheat the oven to 230°C.

Arrange the trout in a shallow dish and cover with the mushroom mixture. Sprinkle with the breadcrumbs. Combination bake at 230°C using 30% (low) microwave power for 10 minutes. Serve hot.

Cod, tomato and mushroom pie

Microwave only: 100% (high)
Combination bake: 200°C using 30% (low)

Serves: 4
Total cooking time: 40 minutes

675g/1½lb potatoes, peeled and sliced
8 tbsp water
25g/1oz butter
1–2 tbsp milk
1 bunch spring onions, trimmed and finely chopped
salt and pepper
2 tbsp oil
275g/10oz closed cup mushrooms, wiped and sliced
4 tbsp flour
300ml/½ pint milk
½ tsp paprika
225g/8oz tomatoes, peeled and sliced
450g/1lb cod fillet, skinned, boned and cut into large pieces

Place the potatoes and water in a bowl. Cover and microwave at 100% (high) microwave only for 12 minutes, stirring once, until tender. Drain and mash with the butter, milk, spring onions and salt and pepper to taste until smooth and fluffy.

Place the oil and mushrooms in a bowl. Cover and microwave at 100% (high) microwave only for 3 minutes. Add the flour, blending well, then gradually add the milk, paprika and salt and pepper to taste. Cover and microwave at 100% (high) microwave only for 5 minutes, stirring every 1 minute, until smooth, boiling and thickened.

Preheat the oven to 200°C.

Place the cod in a deep ovenproof dish. Top with the tomatoes then pour over the sauce. Pipe or spoon the potato mixture over the top and fork lightly. Combination bake at 200°C using 30% (low) for 20 minutes, until golden and the fish is cooked and flaky. Serve hot.

Chicken mille-feuille

Combination bake: 250°C using 50% (medium)
Serves: 4
Total cooking time: 5½–6½ minutes

250g/8¾oz packet frozen puff pastry, thawed

beaten egg or milk to glaze
Filling:
275g/10oz cooked boneless chicken, diced
½ small green pepper, cored, seeded and chopped
½ small red pepper, cored, seeded and chopped
2 tsp capers, chopped (optional)
50g/2oz Danish Mellow Blue cheese or other soft blue-veined cheese
4 tsp mayonnaise
2 tbsp natural thick set yogurt or soured cream
salt and pepper
pinch of ground paprika
lemon juice
cucumber twists to garnish

Preheat the oven to 250°C. Roll out the pastry, on a lightly floured surface, to an oblong measuring 23 × 38cm/9 × 15in. Trim and cut into three equal pieces measuring 23 × 13cm/9 × 5in. Prick the pastry pieces thoroughly with a fork and mark one in a lattice pattern (this will form the top layer of the mille-feuille). Chill for 10 minutes then place each either on an oblong microwave baking dish that will fit your oven or on pieces of greaseproof paper that are slightly larger than the pastry pieces for baking.

The pastries must be cooked two at a time – place one directly on the turntable or base of the oven and the second on the wire rack above. Combination bake at 250°C using 50% (medium) microwave power for 3 minutes. At this point the pastry on the rack should be well puffed and golden brown. Remove and leave to cool on a cooling rack. Transfer the pastry from the turntable to the wire rack and place the remaining third pastry piece on the turntable or base of the oven. Continue to combination bake at 250°C using 50% (medium) microwave power for a further 1–1½ minutes. Remove the pastry from the wire rack which should now be well puffed and golden brown and cool as before Transfer the final pastry piece from the turntable or base of the oven to the wire rack to finish cooking for a final 1½- 2 minutes. Remove and allow to cool thoroughly.

Meanwhile, mix the chicken with the peppers and capers if used. Beat the cheese until softened then add the mayonnaise, yogurt or soured cream, salt and pepper to taste, paprika and lemon juice to taste. Fold into the chicken mixture.

Trim the edges of the pastry pieces so they are all the same size. Place one piece of pastry on a serving dish and cover with half of the chicken mixture. Place a second piece of pastry on top and cover with the remaining chicken mixture. Finally cover with the lattice-marked pastry piece.

Chill lightly before serving garnished with cucumber twists.

Speedy chicken and vegetable pie

Microwave only: 100% (high)
Combination bake: 250°C using 50% (medium)
Serves: 4
Total cooking time: 19–22 minutes

450g/1lb uncooked diced chicken
1 onion, peeled and finely chopped
1 carrot, peeled and grated
50g/2oz mushrooms, wiped and sliced
15g/½oz butter
1 tbsp plain flour
2 small cans chicken noodle soup
100g/4oz frozen peas
1 tbsp chopped parsley
1 bay leaf
salt and pepper
175g/6oz shortcrust pastry (made with 175g/6oz plain flour, 75g/3oz butter
    or margarine and 2–3 tbsp water)
beaten egg to glaze

Place the chicken, onion, carrot, mushrooms and butter in a medium-sized pie dish. Cover and microwave at 100% (high) microwave only for 7 minutes, stirring twice. Add the flour, blending well. Stir in the soup, peas, parsley, bay leaf and salt and pepper to taste, blending well.

Preheat the oven to 250°C.

Roll out the prepared pastry, on a lightly floured surface, to an oval or round about 4cm/1½in larger than the pie dish. Trim a 2.5cm/1in strip from the edge of the pastry to make a pastry collar. Moisten the pie dish rim with water and press the pastry collar firmly on to the rim, overlapping the ends. Dampen the pastry collar with water then top with the pastry lid and press firmly together. Trim away any excess pastry with a knife and knock up the crust to seal. Flute the edges of the pie and decorate with any pastry trimmings if liked. Glaze with beaten egg.

Combination bake at 250°C using 50% (medium) microwave power for 12–15 minutes, or until the pastry is cooked and browned and the chicken is tender. Serve hot.

Savoury minced beef popovers

Microwave only: 100% (high)
Combination bake: 250°C using 50% (medium)
Serves: 6
Total cooking time: 34 minutes

Batter:
2 tbsp oil
100g/4oz plain flour, sifted
pinch of salt
2 eggs
300ml/½ pint milk
Filling:
1 onion, peeled and finely chopped
450g/1lb minced beef
1 tbsp plain flour
4 tbsp horseradish relish
1 tbsp tomato purée
225g/8oz frozen mixed vegetables
5 tbsp beef stock
salt and pepper

Oil six large individual ramekin dishes. Mix the flour with the salt in a bowl. Make a well in the centre, add the eggs and mix to a smooth batter, gradually adding the milk. Leave to stand while cooking the filling.

Place the onion in a bowl. Cover and microwave at 100% (high) microwave only for 3 minutes, stirring once. Add the minced beef, cover and microwave at 100% (high)

microwave only, for 8 minutes, stirring to break up every
2 minutes. Add the flour, blending well. Stir in the
horseradish relish, tomato purée, vegetables, stock and salt
and pepper to taste, blending well. Cover and microwave at
100% (high) microwave only for 8 minutes, stirring twice.
Leave to stand, covered, while preparing the popovers.

Preheat the oven to 250°C.

Divide the batter between the ramekins and combination
bake at 250°C using 50% (medium) microwave power for
15 minutes, or until well risen and golden brown. Remove
from the oven and immediately fill with the minced beef
mixture. Serve at once with a little creamed potato if liked.

Meatloaf

Combination bake: 250°C using 50% (medium)
Serves: 4–6
Total cooking time: 18–20 minutes

675g/1½lb minced beef
1 onion, peeled and finely chopped
2 tbsp tomato purée
100g/4oz fresh white or brown breadcrumbs
1 tbsp Worcestershire sauce
2 tsp dried mixed herbs
1 garlic clove, peeled and crushed (optional)
salt and pepper

Mix the beef with the onion, tomato purée, breadcrumbs,
Worcestershire sauce, herbs, garlic if used and salt and
pepper to taste, blending well.

Spoon into a 450g/1lb loaf dish and combination bake at
250°C using 50% (medium) microwave power for 18–20
minutes, or until browned and cooked through. Allow to
stand for 5 minutes before serving hot with vegetables in
season. Alternatively leave to cool then serve cold, cut into
slices with salad.

Last-minute lasagne

Microwave only: 100% (high)
Combination bake: 200°C using 50% (medium)
Serves: 4–6
Total cooking time: 42½–48 minutes

1 large onion. peeled and chopped
1 garlic clove, peeled and crushed
1 green pepper cored. seeded and chopped
450g/1lb minced beef
400g/14oz can chopped tomatoes
2 tbsp tomato purée
4 tbsp red wine or beef stock
1 tsp dried marjoram
1 tsp dried basil
salt and pepper
40g/1½oz butter
3 tbsp flour
450ml/¾ pint milk
75g/3oz Cheddar cheese, grated
175g/6oz no-need-to-precook lasagne
2 tbsp dry breadcrumbs
2 tbsp grated Parmesan cheese

Place the onion, garlic and green pepper in a bowl. Cover and microwave at 100% (high) microwave only for 3 minutes. Add the minced beef and microwave at 100% (high) microwave only for 4 minutes, stirring twice to break up any lumps. Stir in the tomatoes, tomato purée, red wine or stock, marjoram, basil and salt and pepper to taste, blending well. Cover and microwave at 100% (high) microwave only for 6 minutes, stirring twice.

To make a cheese sauce, place the butter in a large jug or bowl and microwave at 100% (high) microwave only for ½ minute to melt. Add the flour then blend in the milk. Microwave at 100% (high) microwave only for 4–4½ minutes, stirring every 1 minute until the sauce is smooth, boiling and thickened. Stir in the grated Cheddar cheese and salt and pepper to taste, blending well.

Preheat the oven to 200°C.

Layer the lasagne with the beef mixture in a large round

or square dish that will comfortably fit in the oven, finishing with a layer of pasta. Cover with the cheese sauce. Mix the breadcrumbs with the Parmesan and sprinkle over the top. Combination bake at 200°C using 50% (medium) microwave power for 25–30 minutes, until cooked and golden.

Serve hot with a crisp newly tossed green salad.

Meatball toad-in-the-hole

Combination bake: 250°C using 50% (medium)
Serves: 4
Total cooking time: 20 minutes

450g/1lb minced beef
1 tbsp Worcestershire sauce
1 tbsp snipped chives
½ small onion, peeled and chopped
salt and pepper
100g/4oz plain flour
2 eggs
300ml/½ pint milk

Mix the beef with the Worcestershire sauce, chives, onion and salt and pepper to taste, blending well. Divide and shape into about 20 small meatballs. Place in a 25cm/10in flan dish and combination bake at 250°C using 50% (medium) microwave power for 5 minutes.

Meanwhile, sift the flour and a pinch of salt into a bowl Make a well in the centre and crack in the eggs. Gradually beat the eggs into the flour, adding the milk to make a smooth batter.

Drain any excess fat from the meatballs then add the batter, pouring it carefully around the meatballs. Return to the oven and combination bake at 250°C using 50% (medium) microwave power for a further 15 minutes, until well risen, crisp and golden brown. Serve at once.

Variation:

Traditional toad-in-the-hole

Prepare as above but use 450g/1lb skinless sausages instead of the meatball mixture. The sausages need not be pre-browned if liked and can be cooked in the batter at 250°C using 50% (medium) microwave power for 20 minutes, until well risen, golden, crisp and light.

Beef spice hot-pot

Combination bake: 170°C using 30% (low)
Serves: 4–6
Total cooking time: 1 hour 10 minutes

675g/1½lb shin or skirt of beef, cubed
100g/4oz streaky bacon
2 onions, peeled and sliced
400g/14oz can chopped tomatoes
2 tbsp tomato purée
2 tbsp ground paprika
pinch of cayenne pepper
½ tsp dried thyme
1½ tsp mustard powder
salt and pepper
175g/6oz button mushrooms, wiped
300ml/½ pint pale ale

Brown the meat conventionally in a frying pan if liked. Place in a large casserole dish with the bacon, onions, tomatoes, tomato purée, paprika, cayenne pepper, thyme, mustard powder, salt and pepper to taste, mushrooms and pale ale, blending well.

Cover and combination bake at 170°C using 30% (low) for 1 hour 10 minutes until tender, stirring halfway through the cooking time.

Serve hot with jacket potatoes, boiled rice or noodles.

Buckingham liver roly-poly

Microwave only: 100% (high)
Combination bake: 200°C using 50% (medium)
Serves: 6
Total cooking time: 21–24 minutes

175g/6oz streaky bacon, rinded and chopped
225g/8oz pig's or lamb's liver, diced
1 onion, peeled and chopped
½ tsp dried sage
2 tsp chopped parsley
salt and pepper
Pastry:
225g/8oz self-raising flour
100g/4oz shredded suet
150ml/¼ pint water
beaten egg to glaze

Place the bacon, liver, onion and sage in a bowl. Cover and microwave at 100% (high) microwave only for 6–7 minutes, stirring twice, until no longer pink and the onion is softened. Add the parsley and salt and pepper to taste, blending well.

Preheat the oven to 200°C.

To make the pastry, mix the flour with the suet and a pinch of salt. Stir in the water to make a pliable soft dough. Knead until smooth then roll out, on a lightly floured surface, to a rectangle measuring 23 × 35cm/9 × 12in. Spread the liver filling over the pastry, almost to the edges. Roll up the pastry from the shortest end and seal the edges to enclose the filling.

Place, seam side down, on a large flan dish or ovenproof plate and glaze with beaten egg. Combination bake at 200°C using 50% (medium) microwave power for 15–17 minutes, or until the pastry is well risen, golden brown and the filling is cooked.

Serve hot, cut into slices with boiled potatoes and carrots.

Pork and tarragon pasties

Microwave only: 100% (high)
Combination bake: 220°C using 50% (medium)
Serves: 4
Total cooking time: 25–27 minutes

350g/12oz pork shoulder, chopped
50g/2oz unsmoked back bacon, rinded and chopped
1 tbsp oil
1 onion, peeled and chopped
50g/2oz mushrooms, wiped and sliced
1 tbsp tomato purée
2 tsp dried tarragon
2 tsp flour
salt and pepper
225g/8oz shortcrust pastry (made with 225g/8oz plain flour, 100g/4oz
   butter or margarine and 4 tbsp cold water)
beaten egg to glaze

Place the pork, bacon, oil and onion in a bowl. Cover and
microwave at 100% (high) microwave only for 5 minutes,
stirring twice. Add the mushrooms, tomato purée, tarragon,
flour and salt and pepper to taste, blending well. Cover
and microwave at 100% (high) microwave only for 2
minutes, stirring once. Allow to cool.

Preheat the oven to 220°C.

Roll out the pastry, on a lightly floured surface, and cut
out four 20cm/8in rounds. Divide the meat mixture between
the circles. Dampen the pastry edges with water and draw
the rounds up to make a seam across the top. Crimp the
edges decoratively and brush with beaten egg to glaze. Place
equally on two ovenproof plates or shallow dishes. Place
one on the turntable or base of the oven and the other on
the wire rack above. Combination bake at 220°C using
50% (medium) microwave power for 12 minutes.

Exchange the pasties from the wire rack to the turntable
or base of the oven and those that have been cooking on
the turntable or base to the wire rack and continue to
combination bake at 220°C using 50% (medium)
microwave power for 6–8 minutes, or until cooked, golden
and crisp. Serve hot.

Lamb hotchpotch

Combination bake: 170°C using 100% (high) and
170°C using 30% (low)

Serves: 4

Total cooking time: 40 minutes

25g/1oz butter
1 tbsp oil
675g/1½lb lean lamb, cubed
100g/4oz lamb's kidney, cored and cut into large pieces
40g/1½oz plain flour
300ml/½ pint red wine or meat stock
1 tbsp tomato purée
1 bouquet garni
salt and pepper
175g/6oz mushrooms, wiped
175g/6oz baby onions, peeled
chopped parsley to garnish

Heat the butter and oil in a frying pan and sauté the lamb
and kidney until browned on all sides. Alternatively,
preheat a large browning dish according to the
manufacturer's instructions, about 6 minutes at 100%
(high) microwave only, add the butter and oil and
microwave at 100% (high) microwave only for ½ minute.
Add the lamb and kidney and turn quickly on all sides to
brown evenly.

Remove the meat and place in a large casserole dish. Stir
the flour into the meat juices, blending well. Gradually add
the stock or wine, tomato purée, bouquet garni and salt and
pepper to taste. Pour over the meat and mix to blend.

Combination bake at 170°C using 100% (high) microwave
power for 5 minutes. Reduce the microwave level to 30%
(low) and combination bake for a further 35 minutes, adding
the mushrooms and onions after 20 minutes, stirring twice.
Serve hot garnished with chopped parsley.

Variation:

Lamb and bean hot potch

Prepare and cook as above but add a 425g/15oz can baked beans to the lamb mixture before cooking, blending well. This recipe will stretch to serve 6.

Filo spinach pie

Microwave only: 100% (high)
Combination bake: 190°C using 30% (low)
Serves: 4
Total cooking time: 30–32 minutes

450g/1lb fresh spinach, trimmed and washed
2 tbsp oil
2 onions, peeled and chopped
½ tsp ground cumin
2 tbsp chopped parsley
salt and pepper
4 eggs, beaten
175g/6oz Feta cheese, crumbled
50g/2oz Cheddar cheese, grated
4 tbsp natural yogurt
100g/4oz butter, melted
16 sheets filo pastry

Place the spinach in a dish without any additional water. Cover and microwave at 100% (high) microwave only for 6–8 minutes, stirring once. Leave to stand for 2 minutes then chop finely.

Place the oil and onions in a bowl. Cover and microwave at 100% (high) microwave only for 4 minutes, stirring once. Add the cumin, parsley, spinach and salt and pepper to taste, blending well. Stir in the eggs, Feta cheese, grated cheese and yogurt, blending well.

Preheat the oven to 190°C.

Liberally brush a medium-sized baking dish with some of the melted butter. Line the base with half of the filo sheets, brushing between each layer with melted butter. Cover with

53

the cheesy spinach filling and top with the remaining filo sheets again brushed with melted butter. Pour any remaining butter over the top of the pie, brushing well to coat evenly.

Combination bake at 190°C using 30% (low) microwave power for 20 minutes, or until crisp, golden and cooked. Serve hot cut into thick squares.

Celery, ham and cheese poppyseed plait

Microwave only: 100% (high)
Combination bake: 250°C using 50% (medium)
Serves: 6
Total cooking time: 15–18 minutes

25g/1oz butter
1 stick celery, scrubbed and finely chopped
2 medium leeks, trimmed, washed and sliced
150g/5oz cooked ham, chopped
50g/2oz fresh breadcrumbs
50g/2oz Danish Blue cheese, crumbled
pinch of dried sage
1 egg, beaten
salt and pepper
Pastry:
225g/8oz wheatmeal flour
100g/4oz butter
4 tbsp water
poppyseeds to sprinkle

Place the butter in a bowl with the celery and leeks. Cover and microwave at 100% (high) microwave only for 3 minutes, stirring once. Add the ham, breadcrumbs, cheese, sage, half of the egg and salt and pepper to taste, blending well.

Preheat the oven to 250°C.

To make the pastry, sift the flour into a bowl, adding any bran left in the sieve. Rub in the butter until the mixture resembles fine breadcrumbs. Stir in the water and bind to a firm but pliable dough. Roll out the pastry, on a lightly floured surface, to a rectangle measuring about 25 × 30cm/ 12 × 10in.

Spoon the ham mixture down the centre of the plait, leaving a 5cm/2in border at the short edges. Make cuts into the pastry, from the long edges at 2.5cm/1in intervals ready for plaiting. Brush the pastry with the remaining beaten egg and plait over the filling by crossing alternate strips of pastry from either side over the filling and pressing down lightly to seal. Glaze with beaten egg and sprinkle with poppyseeds.

Place on a large flan dish or ovenproof plate and combination bake at 250°C using 50% (medium) microwave power for 12–15 minutes, or until dark golden and cooked through.

Serve warm, cut into thick slices, with a crisp salad and tomato chutney.

Combination roasting guide for meat, poultry and game

Meat, poultry or game		Temperature	Microwave power level	Minutes per 450g/1lb	Guidelines
Beef:	topside, sirloin and rolled rib	180°C	medium	12–14	Place in dish or on rack. Turn over halfway through cooking time. Leave to stand 10 minutes before carving.
		220°C	low	10–12	
	or				
	rump steak – medium	240°C	medium	5	Place in dish or on rack. Turn over halfway through cooking time.
Lamb:	leg and shoulder joints	200°C	medium	9–12	Place in dish. Turn over halfway through cooking time. Baste regularly. Leave to stand 10 minutes before carving.
		200°C	low	18–22	
	or				
	4 lamb chops	240°C	medium	7–9	Place in dish. Turn over halfway through cooking time.
		200°C	low	12–14	
	or				
	lamb leg steaks	240°C	medium	10–12	
	boned and rolled breast joint	220°C	medium	13–14	Place in dish. Turn over halfway through cooking time. Baste regularly. Leave to stand 10 minutes before carving.

Meat, poultry or game		Temperature	Microwave power level	Minutes per 450g/1lb	Guidelines
Pork:	loin and leg joints	220°C then 190°C	medium	14–16	Reduce temperature after 15 minutes then increase again for last 5 minutes to crisp any crackling. Turn twice during cooking. Leave to stand 10 minutes before carving.
	or	200°C	low	20–22	As above without reducing temperature.
	4 chops	240°C	medium	7–9	Place in dish. Turn over halfway through cooking time.
	or	220°C	low	12–14	
	belly of pork	240°C	medium	10	Turn over twice during cooking time. Leave to stand 10 minutes before carving.
Gammon:	joints	200°C then 180°C	medium	15–18	Place in a deep dish and almost but not quite cover with boiling water. Add seasonings. Turn twice during cooking. Reduce temperature halfway through cooking time.
Chicken:	whole	220°C	medium	7–9	Place in a dish and dot with butter and seasonings. Turn twice during cooking. Leave to stand 10 minutes before carving.
	or	200°C	low	12–15	
	4 quarters	200°C	low	16–20	Turn over once during cooking time.
	4 pieces, e.g. drumsticks, thighs	200°C	low	12–15	Turn over once during cooking time.

Meat, poultry or game		Temperature	Microwave power level	Minutes per 450g/1lb	Guidelines
Duck:	whole or	240°C 220°C	medium medium	7–8 8–10	Prick skin, place in a dish, turn twice removing excess fat. Leave to stand 10 minutes before carving.
Turkey:	whole or	200°C 220°C	medium low	6–7 8	Place in a dish, turn twice during cooking, basting regularly. Leave to stand 15 minutes before carving.
Pheasant:	1 brace	200°C	low	30–35 total cooking time	Bard well with bacon. Turn over twice during cooking time. Leave to stand 10 minutes.
Pigeon:	4	190°C	low	25–30 total cooking time	Bard or baste well. Turn over twice during cooking time. Leave to stand 10 minutes.
Other game birds:	e.g. quail, guinea fowl, etc.	200°C	low	9–10	Bard or baste well. Turn over twice during cooking time. Leave to stand 10 minutes.

Note: Preheat the oven if calculated cooking time is less tnan 30 minutes. No need to preheat if times are more. Also see specific recipe instructions.

Vegetables

Oven crispy jacket baked potatoes

Combination bake: 250°C using 100% (high)
Serves: 4
Total cooking time: 13–15 minutes

4 × 175g/6oz potatoes
oil

Scrub the potatoes, prick the skins and brush with oil. Place
on the oven rack and combination bake at 250°C using
100% (high) for 13–15 minutes. Ideally preheat the oven
before cooking for a really crisp result.

Allow to stand for 3 minutes before serving split and filled
with butter or soured cream.

To cook 1 × 175g/6oz potato – 250°C using 100% (high) –
5–6 minutes
To cook 2 × 175g/6oz potatoes – 250°C using 100% (high)
– 7–8 minutes
To cook 3 × 175g/6oz potatoes – 250°C using 100% (high)
– 9–12 minutes

Cheese and bacon stuffed jacket potatoes

Microwave only: 100% (high)
Combination bake: 250°C using 100% (high)
Serves: 4
Total cooking time: 33–39 minutes

225g/8oz middlecut bacon rashers, rinded
50g/2oz butter
1 onion, peeled and chopped
4 large baking potatoes, scrubbed and pricked
100g/4oz Samsoe cheese, grated
salt and pepper

Place the bacon on a plate and microwave at 100% (high)
microwave only for 6–8 minutes, turning over once, until
cooked. Drain on absorbent kitchen towel. Separate the
rashers into back and streaky and chop the back leaving
the streaky whole.

60

Place a quarter of the butter and the onion in a bowl and microwave at 100% (high) microwave only for 3 minutes, stirring once.

Place the potatoes on the wire rack in the oven and combination bake at 250°C using 100% (high) microwave power for 22–25 minutes, until cooked and tender. Cut the top third off each potato and scoop the flesh into a bowl, leaving the skins intact. Mash the potato coarsely and add 75g/3oz of the cheese, the cooked onion mixture, chopped bacon, remaining butter and salt and pepper to taste, blending well. Return the mixture to the potato skins, piling the mixture high and top with the streaky bacon rashers and remaining cheese.

Return to the oven and combination bake at 250°C using 100% (high) microwave power for 2–3 minutes until crisp and golden.

Serve hot with a crisp green salad.

Lyonnaise potato, onion and ham sausage bake

Combination bake: 220°C using 50% (medium)
Serves: 4
Total cooking time: 22–25 minutes

450g/1lb potatoes, peeled and thinly sliced
2 onions, peeled and sliced into rings
100g/4oz ham sausage, sliced
salt and pepper
25g/1oz butter
4 tbsp milk
2 tbsp single cream or top of the milk
pinch of ground nutmeg
chopped parsley to garnish

Layer the potatoes, onions and ham sausage in a medium sized baking dish, seasoning liberally between each layer with salt and pepper. Dot with the butter. Blend the milk with the cream and nutmeg and pour over the potato mixture.

Combination bake at 220°C using 50% (medium) microwave power for 22–25 minutes, or until the potatoes are cooked fork tender and the topping is crisp and golden brown.

Serve hot sprinkled with chopped parsley. A delicious dish to eat on its own but tasty as an accompaniment to meat.

Swiss rosti

Combination bake: 200°C using 30% (low)
Serves: 4–6
Total cooking time: 25 minutes

25g/1oz butter
1kg/2lb potatoes, peeled and grated
1 small onion, peeled and grated
salt and pepper
50g/2oz Gruyère cheese, grated

Spread the butter over the base and sides of a 20cm/8in round or oval ovenproof dish. Mix the potatoes with the onion and season with salt and pepper to taste.

Place half of the potato mixture in the dish and cover with the grated cheese. Top with the remaining potato and onion mixture.

Combination bake at 200°C using 30% (low) for 25 minutes until golden, crisp and tender. Serve hot with roasts and grills.

Cauliflower cheese

Microwave only: 100% (high)
Combination bake: 250°C using 50% (medium)
Serves: 4
Total cooking time: 21–22 minutes

450g/1lb cauliflower florets
2 tbsp water
25g/1oz butter
25g/1oz plain flour
300ml/½ pint milk
100g/4oz Cheddar cheese, grated
salt and pepper

Place the cauliflower and water in a medium-sized casserole dish. Cover and microwave at 100% (high) microwave only for 10 minutes, stirring once. Remove and drain thoroughly.

Place the butter in a jug and microwave at 100% (high) microwave only for 1 minute to melt. Blend in the flour and milk. Microwave at 100% (high) microwave only, for 3 minutes, stirring every 1 minute, until boiling, smooth and thickened. Stir in half of the cheese, blending well.

Pour the sauce over the cauliflower to coat and sprinkle with the remaining cheese. Combination bake at 250°C using 50% (medium) microwave power for 7–8 minutes, or until golden, cooked and bubbly.

Alternative method

The above recipe can also be cooked at combination bake 250°C using 100% (high) microwave power for 5 minutes if preferred

Stuffed onions

Microwave only: 100% (high)
Combination bake: 200°C using 30% (low)
Serves: 4
Total cooking time: 29–34 minutes

4 × 175g 6oz Spanish onions
50g 2oz butter
50g 2oz breadcrumbs
25g 1oz chopped mixed nuts
50g/2oz Caerphilly cheese, grated
1 tbsp sunflower seeds
1 tbsp chopped parsley
salt and pepper
2 tbsp water

Carefully peel the onions leaving most of the root intact. Hollow out the centres using a small sharp knife. Chop half of the scooped out onion and place in a bowl with the butter. (Use the remaining onion for another dish.)

Microwave at 100% (high) microwave only for 4 minutes, stirring once.

Add the breadcrumbs, nuts, cheese, sunflower seeds, parsley and salt and pepper to taste, blending well. Spoon back into the onions and place in a large casserole dish. Add the water, cover and combination bake at 200°C using 30% (low) for 25–30 minutes, or until the onions are tender.

Serve hot with roast meat and poultry or as part of a vegetarian style meal.

Mid-winter root vegetable ring

Microwave only: 100% (high)
Combination bake: 200°C using 30% (low)
Serves: 4
Total cooking time: 20½–22½ minutes

450g/1lb mixed carrots, swede, parsnip and turnip, peeled and diced
2 tbsp water
40g/1½oz butter
25g/1oz flour
4 tbsp milk or milk and cream mixed
2 eggs, separated
salt and pepper
1 tbsp chopped parsley

Place the vegetables in a bowl with the water. Cover and microwave at 100% (high) microwave only for 6–8 minutes, or until tender. Drain and purée in a blender or pass through a fine sieve.

Place the butter in a bowl and microwave at 100% (high) microwave only for 1 minute to melt. Blend in the flour and milk or milk and cream mixture. Microwave at 100% (high) microwave only for 1½ minutes, stirring twice. Add the puréed vegetables, egg yolks, salt and pepper to taste and parsley, blending well.

Preheat the oven to 200°C.

Whisk the egg whites until they stand in stiff peaks. Fold into the vegetable mixture with a metal spoon. Pour into a buttered medium-sized ring mould, about 20cm/8in in diameter. Combination bake at 200°C using 30% (low) microwave power for 12 minutes, or until firm to the touch.

Serve hot with a light herby sauce – silky smooth herb or lemon hollandaise sauce is particularly good.

Wholemeal vegetable pie

Microwave only: 100% (high)
Combination bake: 180°C using 30% (low)
Serves: 6
Total cooking time: 26–31 minutes

Pastry:
250g/9oz wholemeal flour
pinch of salt
125g/4½oz mixed butter and white vegetable fat
4 tbsp water
beaten egg to glaze
Filling:
25g/1oz butter or margarine
1 onion, peeled and chopped
1 carrot, peeled and chopped
2 courgettes, trimmed and sliced
175g/6oz broccoli, chopped
100g/4oz cabbage, shredded
½ red pepper, cored, seeded and sliced
2 tsp made mustard
salt and pepper
100g/4oz Cheddar cheese, grated
2 tbsp tomato purée

To make the pastry, sift the flour and salt into a bowl, adding any bran left in the sieve. Rub in the fats until the mixture resembles fine breadcrumbs. Bind to a firm but pliable dough with the water and knead lightly until smooth. Roll out two-thirds of the pastry and use to line a 20cm/8in pie dish.

Place the butter, onion and carrot in a bowl. Cover and microwave at 100% (high) microwave only for 3 minutes. Add the courgettes, broccoli, cabbage, red pepper, mustard and salt and pepper to taste, blending well. Cover and microwave at 100% (high) microwave only for 3 minutes, stirring once. Add half of the cheese and tomato purée, blending well.

Preheat the oven to 180°C.

Spoon the filling into the pie crust. Roll out the remaining pastry to make a lid for the pie. Brush the edges of the pastry rim with water and place the lid in position, pressing down firmly to seal. Trim and crimp the edges and use any pastry trimmings to decorate the pie if liked. Sprinkle with the remaining cheese and combination bake at 180°C using 30% (low) for 20–25 minutes, or until well risen, golden and the vegetables are tender. Serve warm.

Stuffed marrow rings

Microwave only: 100% (high)
Combination bake: 220°C using 50% (medium)
Serves: 4
Total cooking time: 14–16 minutes

1 medium-sized marrow
Stuffing:
1 onion. peeled and sliced
1 stick celery, scrubbed and sliced
25g/1oz butter
100g/4oz mushrooms, wiped and sliced
1 tbsp tomato purée
100g/4oz mixed nuts, chopped
½ tsp powdered cinnamon
½ tsp dried rosemary
50g/2oz Danish Blue cheese, crumbled
75g/3oz fresh breadcrumbs
1 egg, beaten
salt and pepper
rosemary sprigs to garnish

Peel the marrow, cut into four thick rings and scoop out the seeds from the centre. Blanch in boiling water for 2 minutes. Drain and place the rings, cut sides down, into a greased flan dish.

Place the onion, celery and butter in a bowl. Cover and microwave at 100% (high) microwave only for 4 minutes,

66

stirring once. Add the mushrooms and microwave, uncovered, at 100% (high) microwave only for a further 2 minutes. Add the tomato purée, nuts, cinnamon, rosemary, cheese, breadcrumbs, egg and salt and pepper to taste, blending well. Pile the filling equally into the marrow rings.

Combination bake at 220°C using 50% (medium) microwave power for 8–10 minutes, or until the marrow is tender. Serve hot garnished with rosemary sprigs. Delicious served with baked potatoes and green beans.

A–Z of microwave vegetable cooking

A

Artichokes

GLOBE   Discard the tough, outer leaves. Snip the tips off the remaining leaves and trim the stems to the base. Wash and shake to remove excess water, stand upright in a cooking dish. Pour over water (or stock) and lemon juice. Cover and cook for the time specified, basting and rearranging twice. Test if cooked at the minimum time – try to pull a leaf from the base, if it comes away freely the artichoke is cooked. Leave to stand, covered, for 5 minutes before serving.

Quantity	Water	Lemon juice	Power	Minutes
1	6 tbsp	1½ tsp	100% (high)	5–6
2	8 tbsp	1 tbsp	100% (high)	10–11
4	150ml/¼ pint	2 tbsp	100% (high)	15–18

JERUSALEM   Peel and cut into even-sized pieces. Place in a cooking dish with the water or butter. Cover and cook for the time specified, stirring once. Leave to stand, covered, for 3 minutes before serving.

Quantity	Water	or	Butter	Power	Minutes
450g/1lb	4 tbsp		25g/1oz	100% (high)	8–10

Asparagus

FRESH WHOLE SPEARS   Prepare and arrange in a large shallow dish with pointed tips to the centre. Add water, cover and cook for time specified, rearranging spears but still keeping tips to centre after half of the time.

Quantity	Water	Power	Minutes
450g/1lb	125ml/4½fl oz	100% (high)	12–14

FRESH CUT SPEARS   Prepare and place in a large shallow dish. Add water, cover and cook for time specified, stirring once.

Quantity	Water	Power	Minutes
450g/1lb	125ml/4½fl oz	100% (high)	9–11

FROZEN WHOLE SPEARS   Place in a cooking dish with water. Cover and cook for time specified, rearranging once. Leave to stand for 5 minutes before serving.

Quantity	Water	Power	Minutes
450g/1lb	125ml/4½fl oz	100% (high)	9–12

CANNED WHOLE SPEARS   Drain and place in a cooking dish. Cover and cook for time specified, rearranging once.

Quantity	Power	Minutes
1 × 425g/15oz can	100% (high)	3–4

CANNED CUT SPEARS   Drain and place in a cooking dish. Cover and cook for time specified, rearranging once.

Quantity	Power	Minutes
1 × 300g/11oz can	100% (high)	2–2½

Aubergines

FRESH CUBES   Cut unpeeled aubergine into 2cm/¾in cubes. Place in a cooking dish with butter. Cover and cook for time specified, stirring every 3 minutes. Leave to stand, covered, for 4 minutes. Season after cooking.

Quantity	Butter	Power	Minutes
450g/1lb	25g/1oz	100% (high)	7–10

FRESH WHOLE   Peel off stalks, rinse and dry. Brush with a little oil and prick. Place on absorbent kitchen towel and cook for time specified, turning once. Leave to stand for 4 minutes. Scoop out flesh and use as required.

Quantity	Power	Minutes
1 × 225g/8oz	100% (high)	3–4
2 × 225g/8oz	100% (high)	4–6

FROZEN SLICES   Place in a shallow dish. Cover and cook for time specified, stirring 2–3 times. Drain and pat dry to use.

Quantity	Power	Minutes
225g/8oz	20% (defrost)	7
450g/1lb	20% (defrost)	10–13

B

Beans

FRESH GREEN   Place whole or cut beans in a bowl with the water. Cover and cook for the time specified, stirring once. Leave to stand, covered, for 2–3 minutes before serving.

Quantity	Water	Power	Minutes
225g/8oz whole	2 tbsp	100% (high)	8–10
450g/1lb whole	2 tbsp	100% (high)	15–18
225g/8oz cut	2 tbsp	100% (high)	7–9
450g/1lb cut	2 tbsp	100% (high)	12–15

FRESH BABY GREEN WHOLE OR FRENCH WHOLE   Place in a bowl with the water. Cover and cook for the time specified, stirring 3 times. Leave to stand, covered, for 2–3 minutes before serving.

Quantity	Water	Power	Minutes
225g/8oz	2 tbsp	100% (high)	7–9
450g/1lb	2 tbsp	100% (high)	12–15

FRESH SLICED RUNNER BEANS   Place in a bowl with the water. Cover and cook for the time specified, stirring 3–4 times. Leave to stand, covered, for 2–3 minutes before serving.

Quantity	Water	Power	Minutes
225g/8oz	2 tbsp	100% (high)	7–9
450g/1lb	2 tbsp	100% (high)	12–15

FRESH SHELLED BROAD BEANS   Place in a bowl with the water. Cover and cook for the time specified, stirring once. Leave to stand, covered, for 2–3 minutes before serving.

Quantity	Water	Power	Minutes
225g/8oz	5 tbsp	100% (high)	5–7
450g/1lb	100ml/4fl oz	100% (high)	6–10

FROZEN GREEN BEANS   Place in a bowl with the water. Cover and cook for the time specified, stirring once. Leave to stand, covered, for 2–3 minutes before serving.

Quantity	Water	Power	Minutes
225g/8oz whole	2 tbsp	100% (high)	9–10
450g/1lb whole	4 tbsp	100% (high)	14–15
225g/8oz cut	2 tbsp	100% (high)	6–7
450g/1lb cut	4 tbsp	100% (high)	10–12

FROZEN BABY GREEN WHOLE OR FRENCH WHOLE   Place in a bowl with the water. Cover and cook for the time specified, stirring 3 times. Leave to stand, covered, for 2–3 minutes before serving.

Quantity	Water	Power	Minutes
225g/8oz	2 tbsp	100% (high)	8–9
450g/1lb	4 tbsp	100% (high)	13–15

FROZEN SLICED RUNNER BEANS   Place in a bowl with the water. Cover and cook for the time specified, stirring twice. Leave to stand, covered, for 2–3 minutes before serving.

Quantity	Water	Power	Minutes
225g/8oz	2 tbsp	100% (high)	6–7
450g/1lb	4 tbsp	100% (high)	10–12

FROZEN SHELLED BROAD BEANS   Place in a bowl with the water. Cover and cook for the time specified, stirring twice. Leave to stand, covered, for 2–3 minutes before serving.

Quantity	Water	Power	Minutes
225g/8oz	4 tbsp	100% (high)	6–7
450g/1lb	100ml/4fl oz	100% (high)	10–11

CANNED GREEN AND BROAD BEANS   Drain all but liquid

specified. Place in a cooking dish with the liquid. Cover and cook for time specified, stirring once.

Quantity	Liquid	Power	Minutes
1 × 280g/10oz can whole green	2 tbsp	100% (high)	2–3
2 × 280g/10oz cans whole green	2 tbsp	100% (high)	4–5
1 × 280g/10oz can cut green	2 tbsp	100% (high)	2–3
2 × 280g/10oz cans cut green	2 tbsp	100% (high)	4–4½
1 × 280g/10oz can broad	2 tbsp	100% (high)	2
2 × 280g/10oz cans broad	2 tbsp	100% (high)	3

Beetroot

FRESH Wash the beetroot and pierce the skin with a fork but do not peel. Place in a shallow dish with the water, cover loosely and cook for the time specified, rearranging twice. Leave to stand, covered, for 5 minutes before removing skins to serve or use.

Quantity	Water	Power	Minutes
4 medium	3–4 tbsp	100% (high)	14–16

Broccoli

FRESH SPEARS Place spears in a large shallow dish with tender heads to centre of dish. Add water, cover with a lid or vented cling film. Cook for time specified, rotating dish once. Leave to stand, covered, for 2–4 minutes before serving.

Quantity	Water	Power	Minutes
225g/8oz	4 tbsp	100% (high)	4–5
450g/1 lb	4 tbsp	100% (high)	8–9

FRESH PIECES Cut into 2.5 cm/1 inch pieces. Place in a large dish. Add water, cover and cook for time specified, stirring once. Leave to stand, covered, for 3–5 minutes before serving.

Quantity	Water	Power	Minutes
225g/8oz	4 tbsp	100% (high)	4½–5
450g/1lb	4 tbsp	100% (high)	8½–9½

FROZEN SPEARS   Place in a cooking dish with water. Cover and cook for time specified, stirring once. Leave to stand for 2–3 minutes before serving.

Quantity	Water	Power	Minutes
1 × 250g/9oz packet	4 tbsp	100% (high)	7–8
2 × 250g/9oz packets	4 tbsp	100% (high)	14–15

Brussels sprouts

FRESH   Remove outer leaves, trim and cross-cut base. Place in a cooking dish with the water. Cover and cook for the time specified, stirring once. Leave to stand, covered, for 3–5 minutes before serving.

Quantity	Water	Power	Minutes
450g/1lb	4 tbsp	100% (high)	6–7
900g/2lb	8 tbsp	100% (high)	12–14

FROZEN   Place in a cooking dish with the water. Cover and cook for the time specified, stirring once. Leave to stand, covered, for 3–5 minutes before serving.

Quantity	Water	Power	Minutes
450g/1lb	2 tbsp	100% (high)	10–11
900g/2lb	4 tbsp	100% (high)	20–22

C

Cabbage

FRESH   Core and shred and place in a large dish so that the cabbage fits loosely. Add water, cover and cook for the specified time, stirring once. Leave to stand for 2 minutes before serving. Season after cooking.

Quantity	Water	Power	Minutes
225g/8oz	4 tbsp	100% (high)	7–9
450g/1lb	8 tbsp	100% (high)	9–11

FROZEN   Place in a large dish with the water. Cover and cook for the specified time, stirring once. Leave to stand for 2 minutes before serving. Season after cooking.

Quantity	Water	Power	Minutes
225g/8oz	4 tbsp	100% (high)	6–8
450g/1lb	8 tbsp	100% (high)	8–10

Carrots

FRESH BABY WHOLE AND SLICED   Place in a cooking dish with the water. Cover and cook for the time specified, stirring once. Leave to stand, covered, for 3–5 minutes before serving.

Quantity	Water	Power	Minutes
450g/1lb whole	4 tbsp	100% (high)	12–14
450g/1lb sliced	4 tbsp	100% (high)	10–12

FROZEN BABY WHOLE AND SLICED   Place in a cooking dish with the water. Cover and cook for the time specified, stirring once. Leave to stand, covered, for 2–3 minutes before serving.

Quantity	Water	Power	Minutes
450g/1lb whole	2 tbsp	100% (high)	10–12
450g/1lb sliced	2 tbsp	100% (high)	8–10

Cauliflower

FRESH WHOLE   Trim but leave whole and place, floret side down, in a dish with the water. Cover and cook for the time specified, turning over once. Leave to stand for 3–5 minutes before serving.

Quantity	Water	Power	Minutes
1 × 675g/1½lb whole	8 tbsp	50% (medium)	13–17

FRESH FLORETS   Place in a dish with the water. Cover and cook for the time specified, stirring once. Leave to stand for 3 minutes before serving.

Quantity	Water	Power	Minutes
225g/8oz	3 tbsp	100% (high)	7–8
450g/1lb	4 tbsp	100% (high)	10–12

FROZEN FLORETS   To thaw and cook, place in a dish with the water. Cover and cook for the time specified, stirring once. Leave to stand for 2–3 minutes before serving.

Quantity	Water	Power	Minutes
225g/8oz	3 tbsp	100% (high)	5–6
450g/1lb	4 tbsp	100% (high)	8–9

Celery

FRESH SLICED   Slice into 5mm/¼ inch pieces and place in a shallow cooking dish. Add water and butter, cover and cook for the time specified, stirring once. Leave to stand, covered, for 3 minutes before serving.

Quantity	Water	Butter	Power	Minutes
1 head/9 large sticks	2 tbsp	25g/1oz	100% (high)	5–6

FRESH CELERY HEARTS   Halve each heart lengthways and place in a shallow cooking dish. Add water and a knob of butter if liked. Cover and cook for the time specified, turning once. Leave to stand, covered, for 3 minutes before serving.

Quantity	Water	Power	Minutes
4 hearts	2 tbsp	100% (high)	4½–5

Chinese cabbage

FRESH   Slice and place in a large dish so that the cabbage fits loosely. Add water, cover and cook for the time specified, stirring once. Leave to stand for 3–5 minutes before serving. Season after cooking.

Quantity	Water	Power	Minutes
450g/1lb	2–3 tbsp	100% (high)	6–8

Corn on the cob and corn kernels

FRESH UNHUSKED   Arrange on the base of the cooker or on turntable, evenly spaced. Cook for the time specified, rotating and rearranging once. Leave to stand for 5 minutes before removing husk, silky threads and woody base with a sharp knife.

Quantity	Power	Minutes
1 × 175–225g/6–8oz	100% (high)	3–5
2 × 175–225g/6–8oz	100% (high)	6–8
3 × 175–225g/6–8oz	100% (high)	8–10
4 × 175–225g/6–8oz	100% (high)	10–12

FRESH HUSKED   Wrap individually in cling film or place in a dish with 1 tbsp water and cover. Place or arrange evenly in the microwave and cook for the time specified, rotating and rearranging once. Leave to stand, covered, for 3–5 minutes before serving.

Quantity	Power	Minutes
1 × 175–225g/6–8oz	100% (high)	3–4
2 × 175–225g/6–8oz	100% (high)	5–6
3 × 175–225g/6–8oz	100% (high)	7–8
4 × 175–225g/6–8oz	100% (high)	9–10

FROZEN CORN KERNELS   Place in a cooking dish with 4 tbsp water. Cover and cook for the time specified, stirring once. Leave to stand, covered, for 2–3 minutes before serving.

Quantity	Power	Minutes
1 × 283g/10oz packet	100% (high)	5–6
1 × 454g/1lb packet	100% (high)	7–8

CANNED CORN KERNELS   Drain off all but 2 tbsp can juice. Place in a cooking dish with liquid. Cover and cook for time specified, stirring once.

Quantity	Power	Minutes
1 × 298g/10½oz can	100% (high)	2–3
1 × 340g/12oz can	100% (high)	2½–3

CREAMED CORN KERNELS Place in a cooking dish. Cover and cook for time specified, stirring once.

Quantity	Power	Minutes
1 × 298g/10½oz can	100% (high)	2–3
1 × 340g/12oz can	100% (high)	2½–3

Courgettes

FRESH Top and tail and slice thinly. Place in a shallow cooking dish with butter. Cover loosely and cook for the time specified, stirring once. Leave to stand, covered, for 2–3 minutes before serving.

Quantity	Butter	Power	Minutes
225g/8oz	25g/1oz	100% (high)	4–6½
450g/1lb	40g/1½oz	100% (high)	6–8

FROZEN Place in a shallow cooking dish with butter if liked. Cover loosely and cook for the time specified, stirring once. Leave to stand, covered, for 2–3 minutes before serving.

Quantity	Butter	Power	Minutes
450g/1lb	40g/1½oz	100% (high)	7–8

Curly kale

FRESH Remove the thick stalk and stems and shred. Place in a large dish with the water. Cover and cook for the specified time, stirring every 5 minutes. Leave to stand for 2 minutes before serving.

Quantity	Water	Power	Minutes
450g/1lb	150ml/¼ pint	100% (high)	15–17

F

Fennel

FRESH SLICED Place in a cooking dish with the water. Cover and cook for the time specified, stirring once. Leave to stand, covered, for 2–3 minutes before serving.

Quantity	Water	Power	Minutes
450g/1lb	3 tbsp	100% (high)	9–10

L

Leeks

FRESH WHOLE Trim and slit from the top of the white to the green leaves in 2–3 places. Wash thoroughly and place in a cooking dish with the water. Cover and cook for the time specified, rearranging twice. Leave to stand, covered, for 3–5 minutes before serving.

Quantity	Water	Power	Minutes
450g/1lb	3 tbsp	100% (high)	3–5
900g/2lb	5 tbsp	100% (high)	6–8

FRESH SLICED Place in a cooking dish with the water. Cover and cook for the time specified, stirring once. Leave to stand, covered, for 2–3 minutes before serving.

Quantity	Water	Power	Minutes
450g/1lb	3 tbsp	100% (high)	8–10

FROZEN SLICED Place in a cooking dish with the water. Cover and cook for the time specified, stirring once. Leave to stand, covered, for 2–3 minutes before serving.

Quantity	Water	Power	Minutes
225g/8oz	2 tbsp	100% (high)	6
450g/1lb	3 tbsp	100% (high)	11–12

M

Mangetout

FRESH Trim and place in a cooking dish with the water.
Cover and cook for the time specified, stirring once. Leave
to stand, covered, for 2 minutes before serving.

Quantity	Water	Power	Minutes
100g/4oz	1 tbsp	100% (high)	3–4
225g/8oz	2 tbsp	100% (high)	4–5

FROZEN Place in a cooking dish with the water. Cover and
cook for time specified, stirring once.

Quantity	Water	Power	Minutes
1 × 200g/7oz packet	2 tbsp	100% (high)	3–4

Marrow

FRESH Peel, remove seeds and cut into small neat dice.
Place in a cooking dish without any water. Cover loosely
and cook for the time specified, stirring once. Leave to stand,
covered, for 2–3 minutes before serving.

Quantity	Power	Minutes
450g/1lb	100% (high)	7–10

FROZEN To defrost only, place in a cooking dish, cover and
cook for the time specified, stirring once. Drain and pat
dry to use as required.

Quantity	Power	Minutes
225g/8oz	20% (defrost)	4–5
450g/1lb	20% (defrost)	9–10

Mixed vegetables

FROZEN Place in a cooking dish with the water. Cover and
cook for the time specified, stirring once. Leave to stand,
covered, for 2 minutes before serving.

Quantity	Water	Power	Minutes
225g/8oz packet	2 tbsp	100% (high)	4–5
450g/1lb packet	2 tbsp	100% (high)	7–8

Mushrooms

FRESH WHOLE   Trim and wipe mushrooms. Place in a cooking dish with water or butter. Cover and cook for the specified time, stirring twice. Leave to stand for 1–2 minutes before serving. Season to taste after cooking.

Quantity	Butter	or	Water	Power	Minutes
225g/8oz	25g/1oz		2 tbsp	100% (high)	3–4
450g/1lb	40g/1½oz		3 tbsp	100% (high)	4–5

FRESH SLICED   Trim, wipe and slice mushrooms. Place in a cooking dish with water or butter. Cover and cook for the specified time, stirring once. Leave to stand for 1–2 minutes before serving. Season to taste after cooking.

Quantity	Butter	or	Water	Power	Minutes
225g/8oz	25g/1oz		2 tbsp	100% (high)	2–3
450g/1lb	40g/1½oz		3 tbsp	100% (high)	3–4

FROZEN WHOLE BUTTON   To thaw and cook, place in a shallow dish with a knob of butter. Cover and cook for the time specified, stirring twice. Season to taste and serve.

Quantity	Power	Minutes
100g/4oz	100% (high)	3–4
225g/8oz	100% (high)	5–6

O

Okra

FRESH   Top and tail and sprinkle lightly with salt. Leave to drain for 30 minutes. Rinse and place in a cooking dish with the water or butter. Cover and cook for the time specified, stirring once. Leave to stand, covered, for 3 minutes before serving.

Quantity	Water	or	Butter	Power	Minutes
450g/1lb	2 tbsp		25g/1oz	100% (high)	8–10

Onions

FRESH WHOLE   Peel and place in a cooking dish. Cover and cook for the specified time, rearranging and rotating once. Leave to stand, covered, for 2 minutes before serving.

Quantity	Power	Minutes
450g/1lb or 4 medium	100% (high)	10–12

FRESH SLICED   Peel and cut into thin wedges or slices. Place in a cooking dish with the butter and water. Cover loosely and cook for the specified time, stirring once. Leave to stand, covered, for 5 minutes before serving.

Quantity	Butter	Water	Power	Minutes
450g/1lb	25g/1oz	2 tbsp	100% (high)	7–10

FROZEN WHOLE   Place in a cooking dish with the water. Cover and cook for the time specified, stirring once. Leave to stand, covered, for 2–3 minutes before serving.

Quantity	Water	Power	Minutes
100g/4oz packet small whole	6 tbsp	100% (high)	2–3

FROZEN SLICES OR RINGS   Place in a shallow dish, cover and cook for the time specified, stirring twice. Drain to use.

Quantity	Power	Minutes
225g/8oz	20% (defrost)	4–5
450g/1lb	20% (defrost)	8

P

Pak soi (or bok choy cabbage)

FRESH   Slice stalks and leaves and place in a large dish so
that the cabbage fits loosely. Add water, cover and cook
for the time specified, stirring once. Leave to stand for 3–5
minutes before serving. Season after cooking.

Quantity	Water	Power	Minutes
450g/1lb	2 tbsp	100% (high)	6–8

Parsnips

FRESH WHOLE   Peel and prick with a fork. Arrange in a
large shallow dish with tapered ends to centre. Dot with
butter and add water and lemon juice. Cover and cook for
the time specified, rearranging once. Leave to stand,
covered, for 3 minutes before serving.

Quantity	Butter	Water	Lemon juice	Power	Minutes
450g/1lb	15g/½oz	3 tbsp	1 tbsp	100% (high)	9–12

FRESH SLICES   Peel and slice. Place in a cooking dish with
the butter and add water and lemon juice. Cover and cook
for the time specified, stirring twice. Leave to stand, covered,
for 3 minutes before serving.

Quantity	Butter	Water	Lemon juice	Power	Minutes
450g/1lb	15g/½oz	3 tbsp	1 tbsp	100% (high)	9–12

FRESH CUBES   Peel and cut into 1.5cm/½ inch cubes. Place
in a cooking dish with the butter and add water and lemon
juice. Cover and cook for the time specified, stirring twice.
Leave to stand, covered, for 3 minutes before serving.

Quantity	Butter	Water	Lemon juice	Power	Minutes
450g/1lb	15g/½oz	3 tbsp	1 tbsp	100% (high)	9–12

FROZEN WHOLE   To thaw and cook, arrange in a shallow

dish with tapered ends to centre. Cover and cook for the time specified, rearranging once. Toss in butter and seasoning to serve.

Quantity	Power	Minutes
225g/8oz	100% (high)	7–8
450g/1lb	100% (high)	9–10

FROZEN SLICES To thaw and cook, place in a cooking dish, cover and cook for the time specified, stirring twice. Toss in butter and seasoning to taste to serve.

Quantity	Power	Minutes
225g/8oz	100% (high)	6–7
450g/1lb	100% (high)	12–14

FROZEN CUBES To thaw and cook, place in a cooking dish, cover and cook for the time specified, stirring twice. Toss in butter and seasoning to taste to serve.

Quantity	Power	Minutes
225g/8oz	100% (high)	4–5
450g/1lb	100% (high)	7–9

Peas

FRESH Place in a cooking dish with butter and water. Cover and cook for the time specified, stirring once. Leave to stand. covered, for 3–5 minutes before serving.

Quantity	Butter	Water	Power	Minutes
100g 4oz	15g/½oz	2 tsp	100% (high)	3
225g/8oz	25g/1oz	1 tbsp	100% (high)	4–5
450g/1lb	50g/2oz	2 tbsp	100% (high)	6–8

FROZEN Place in a cooking dish with water. Cover and cook for the time specified, stirring once. Leave to stand, covered, for 3 minutes before serving.

Quantity	Water	Power	Minutes
1 × 225g/8oz packet	2 tbsp	100% (high)	4–6
1 × 450g/1lb packet	4 tbsp	100% (high)	6–8

CANNED   Drain all but liquid specified. Place in a cooking dish with liquid. Cover and cook for time specified, stirring once.

Quantity	Liquid	Power	Minutes
1 × 283g/10oz can	1½ tbsp	100% (high)	1–2
1 × 425g/15oz can	2 tbsp	100% (high)	2–3

Peppers

TO BLANCH BEFORE STUFFING   Halve the peppers lengthways if liked or slice off tops to keep whole and remove and discard the seeds. Place in a shallow dish with the water, cover and cook for the time specified, rotating the dish once. Drain to use.

Quantity	Water	Power	Minutes
4 halves or 2 whole	2 tbsp	100% (high)	6–8

TO COOK RINGS OR SLICES FOR HOT SALADS, RICE MIXTURES, ETC.   Core, seed and slice the peppers. Place in a dish with the water, cover and cook for the time specified, stirring once. Leave to stand, covered, for 5 minutes before using.

Quantity	Water	Power	Minutes
4	1 tbsp	100% (high)	5–7

FROZEN   Place diced or sliced peppers in a bowl. Cover and cook for the time specified, stirring twice. Drain to use.

Quantity	Power	Minutes
50g/2oz diced	20% (defrost)	1–1½
50g/2oz sliced	20% (defrost)	2
100g/4oz diced	20% (defrost)	2–2½
100g/4oz sliced	20% (defrost)	2½–3

FROZEN COOKED STUFFED   To thaw and reheat, stand upright on a serving dish. Cover and cook for the time specified, rearranging twice. Cover with foil and leave to stand for 5 minutes before serving.

Quantity	Power	Minutes
2 whole stuffed	100% (high)	5
4 whole stuffed	100% (high)	10

Potatoes

MASHED OR CREAMED POTATOES   Peel potatoes, cut into 1.5cm/½in cubes and place in a cooking dish with water. Cover and cook for the time specified, stirring once. Leave to stand, covered, for 5 minutes. Drain and mash with butter and seasoning to taste.

Quantity	Butter	Water	Power	Minutes
900g/2lb	25g/1oz	75ml/3 fl oz	100% (high)	11–13

NEW POTATOES OR OLD PEELED AND QUARTERED   Scrub new potatoes and scrape if liked. Peel and quarter old potatoes. Place in a cooking dish with the water. Cover and cook for the time specified, stirring once. Leave to stand, covered, for 5 minutes before serving.

Quantity	Water	Power	Minutes
450g/1lb old	4 tbsp	100% (high)	7–10
450g/1lb new	4 tbsp	100% (high)	6–8

JACKET BAKED IN SKINS   Scrub and prick skin. Place on a double sheet of absorbent kitchen towel. Cook for the time specified, turning over once. If cooking more than 2 potatoes arrange in a ring pattern. Leave to stand for 3–4 minutes before serving.

Quantity	Power	Minutes
1 × 175g/6oz	100% (high)	4–6
2 × 175g/6oz	100% (high)	6–8
3 × 175g/6oz	100% (high)	8–12
4 × 175g/6oz	100% (high)	12–15

SWEET POTATOES   Scrub and prick skin. Place on a double sheet of absorbent kitchen towel. Cook for the time specified, turning over once. Leave to stand for 5 minutes before using.

Quantity	Power	Minutes
450g/1lb	100% (high)	4–6

FROZEN NEW BOILED POTATOES   To thaw and reheat, place in a dish, cover and cook for the time specified, stirring twice. Leave to stand for 2 minutes before serving.

Quantity	Power	Minutes
225g/8oz	100% (high)	2½–3
450g/1lb	100% (high)	5–6

S

Spinach

FRESH   Chop or shred and rinse. Place in a dish without any additional water. Cover and cook for the specified time, stirring once. Leave to stand for 2 minutes before serving. Season to taste after cooking.

Quantity	Power	Minutes
450g/1lb	100% (high)	6–8

FROZEN LEAF OR CHOPPED SPINACH   Place in a dish. Cover and cook for the specified time, stirring to break up twice during the cooking. Season to taste after cooking.

Quantity	Power	Minutes
1 × 275g/10oz packet	100% (high)	7–9

Swedes

FRESH   Peel and cut into 1.5cm/½ inch cubes. Place in a cooking dish with the water and butter. Cover and cook for the time specified, stirring twice. Leave to stand, covered, for 4 minutes. Drain and season to serve or mash with butter, cream and seasonings if liked.

Quantity	Butter	Water	Power	Minutes
450g/1lb	15g/½oz	2 tbsp	100% (high)	10–12

FROZEN To thaw and cook cubed swede, place in a cooking dish, cover and cook for the time specified, stirring twice. Toss in butter and seasonings or mash with butter, cream and seasonings if liked.

Quantity	Power	Minutes
225g/8oz	100% (high)	5–6
450g/1lb	100% (high)	8–10

Swiss chard

FRESH Remove and discard the thick stalk and shred. Place in a large cooking dish with water. Cover and cook for the specified time, stirring every 3 minutes. Leave to stand for 2 minutes before serving. Season to taste after cooking.

Quantity	Water	Power	Minutes
450g/1lb	150ml/¼ pint	100% (high)	5½–6½

T

Tomatoes

TO PEEL FRESH Boil 750ml/1¼ pints water conventionally and place in a bowl. Add pricked tomatoes, cover and cook for the time specified. Remove with a slotted spoon, plunge into cold water – the skin will now peel away easily.

Quantity	Power	Minutes
Up to 450g/1lb	100% (high)	½

TO COOK WHOLE AND HALVES Prick whole or halve, arrange in a circle on a plate, cut sides up. Dot with butter and season with salt and pepper to taste. Cook for the time specified according to size and ripeness.

Quantity	Power	Minutes
1 medium	100% (high)	1/2
4 medium	100% (high)	2–2½
4 large (beef)	100% (high)	3½–4

Turnips

FRESH WHOLE   Choose only small to medium turnips. Peel and prick with a fork. Arrange in a ring pattern in a large shallow dish. Dot with the butter and add water. Cover and cook for the time specified, rearranging once. Leave to stand, covered, for 3 minutes before serving.

Quantity	Butter	Water	Power	Minutes
450g/1lb	15g/½oz	3 tbsp	100% (high)	14–16

FRESH SLICES   Peel and slice. Place in a cooking dish with the butter and water. Cover and cook for the time specified, stirring twice. Leave to stand, covered, for 3 minutes before serving.

Quantity	Butter	Water	Power	Minutes
450g/1lb	15g/½oz	3 tbsp	100% (high)	11–12

FRESH CUBES   Peel and cut into 1.5cm/½ inch cubes. Place in a cooking dish with the butter and water. Cover and cook for the time specified, stirring twice. Leave to stand, covered, for 3 minutes before serving.

Quantity	Butter	Water	Power	Minutes
450g/1lb	15g/½oz	3 tbsp	100% (high)	12–14

Special occasion and entertaining main meals

Roast chicken with lemon and mushroom oaty stuffing

Microwave only: 100% (high)
Combination bake: 220°C using 50% (medium) or
                    220°C using 30% (low)

Serves: 4
Total cooking time: 28½–33½ minutes or
                      38½–43½ minutes

25g/1oz butter
225g/8oz closed cup mushrooms, wiped and finely chopped
2 garlic cloves, peeled and crushed
2 tomatoes, peeled and finely chopped
75g/3oz porridge oats
grated rind of ½ lemon
salt and pepper
1.5kg/3½lb oven-ready roasting chicken
2 tbsp lemon shred marmalade
lemon wedges and watercress sprigs to garnish

Place half of the butter in a bowl with the mushrooms and
garlic, cover and microwave at 100% (high) microwave
only for 3½ minutes, stirring once. Add the tomatoes,
porridge oats, half the lemon rind and salt and pepper to
taste, blending well. Allow to cool.

Preheat the oven to 220°C.

Place the stuffing in the body cavity of the chicken or
under the surface skin of the chicken, by loosening the skin
from the breast and thighs like a pocket, then secure the
skin back in position with wooden cocktail sticks.

Cream the remaining butter with the lemon rind and
smear over the surface skin of the chicken. Place in a
cooking dish and combination bake at 220°C using 50%
(medium) microwave power for 25–30 minutes, or at 220°C
using 30% (low) microwave power for 35–40 minutes,
brushing with the marmalade halfway through the cooking
time, or until the chicken is cooked, golden and the juices
from the thickest parts of the bird, the thighs, run clear.

Serve hot garnished with lemon wedges and watercress
sprigs.

Baked blue cheese chicken surprise

Combination bake: 250°C using 50% (medium)
Serves: 4
Total cooking time: 17–20 minutes

75g/3oz Danish Blue cheese
4 boneless chicken breasts, skinned
25g/1oz plain flour
1 egg, beaten
150g/5oz breadcrumbs made from day old bread
lime or lemon slices and parsley sprigs to garnish

Divide and shape the cheese into 4 thick fingers by gently
moulding with the hands. Make a deep slit into the centre
of each chicken breast with a sharp knife and fill with a
finger of cheese. Press back the chicken meat to enclose the
cheese and coat in the flour. Dip in the beaten egg then coat
completely in breadcrumbs – pressing the crumbs on firmly
to ensure a good coating. Cover and chill for at least 1 hour
for the coating to 'set'.

Preheat the oven to 250°C.

Place the chicken breasts on a greased flan or baking dish
and combination bake at 250°C using 50% (medium)
microwave power for 17–20 minutes, or until cooked, crisp
and golden.

Serve at once garnished with lime or lemon slices and
parsley sprigs. When cut the chicken breasts will reveal a
delicious trickle of mild, blue sauce. Serve with a crisp salad
or vegetables in season.

Variation:

Garlic and herb baked chicken surprise

If liked the blue cheese filling may be replaced with 75g/3oz
herb, garlic and black pepper flavoured butter. Shape into
4 portions and chill thoroughly before placing inside the
chicken breasts.

Herby chicken vol-au-vent

Combination bake: 250°C using 50% (medium)
Serves: 4
Total cooking time: 5½–7 minutes

370g/13oz packet frozen puff pastry, thawed
beaten egg
Filling:
175g/6oz full fat soft cheese with herbs and spices
4 tbsp natural yogurt
2 tbsp milk
275g/10oz cooked boneless chicken, chopped
½ red pepper, cored, seeded and chopped
salt and pepper
parsley or watercress sprigs to garnish

Divide the pastry into two equal pieces and roll out each, on a lightly floured surface, to a 20cm/8in round. From one round cut a 14cm/5½in circle from the centre and reserve as the lid. Place the large uncut circle on a dampened flan dish and brush with water. Top with the pastry ring, pressing it neatly to seal onto the base. Prick the middle of the vol-au-vent and chill for at least 15 minutes. Place the lid on a small ovenproof plate and chill.

Preheat the oven to 250°C.

Glaze the pastry lid and the vol-au-vent ring with beaten egg, taking care not to glaze the sides (this can prevent the pastry from rising). Place the lid on the turntable or base of the oven and the vol-au-vent case on the wire rack above.

Combination bake at 250°C using 50% (medium) microwave power for 4–5 minutes by which time the case should be cooked, flaky and golden. Remove from the oven and leave to cool on a wire rack. Transfer the lid to the wire rack and combination bake at 250°C using 50% (medium) microwave power for a further 1½–2 minutes until cooked, puffy and golden. Allow to cool on a wire rack.

Meanwhile to make the filling, beat the cheese to soften then add the yogurt and milk, blending well. Add the chicken, salt and pepper to taste, blending well. Spoon into cold vol-au-vent case. Garnish with parsley or watercress sprigs to serve.

Tandoori chicken with minted yogurt

Combination bake: 220°C using 30% (low)
Serves: 4
Total cooking time: 20–25 minutes

4 chicken quarter portions, skinned
1 garlic clove, peeled and crushed
2 tsp garam masala
1 tsp ground ginger
1 tsp ground coriander
½ tsp ground cumin
2 tsp tomato purée
2 tbsp lemon juice
1 tsp hot chilli powder
salt and pepper
150ml/¼ pint natural yogurt
½ small green chilli, seeded and finely chopped
2 tsp chopped fresh mint
lettuce leaves, onion rings and lemon slices to garnish

Pierce the flesh of the chicken in several places with a sharp
knife. Mix the garlic with the garam masala, ginger,
coriander, cumin, tomato purée, lemon juice, chilli powder
and salt and pepper to taste. Blend in half of the yogurt
and mix well to a thick paste. Place the chicken in a shallow
roasting dish and liberally coat with the marinade. Leave
to stand for 1 hour for the flavours to permeate the flesh.

Combination bake at 220°C using 30% (low) microwave
power for 20–25 minutes, turning three times, until tender
and cooked.

Meanwhile, mix the remaining yogurt with the chilli, mint
and salt and pepper to taste.

Serve the tandoori chicken on a bed of lettuce leaves,
garnished with onion rings and lemon slices. Serve with
the minted yogurt drizzled over.

Chicken with blue Brie and cucumber sauce

Microwave only: 100% (high)
Combination bake: 250°C using 50% (medium)

Serves: 4
Total cooking time: 21–24 minutes

4 × 225g/8oz boneless chicken breasts, skinned
25g/1oz butter
salt and pepper
Sauce:
25g/1oz butter
1 cucumber, peeled, seeded and chopped
150g/5oz blue Brie cheese, rinded and chopped
1 tsp cornflour
2 tbsp milk
pinch of ground nutmeg
lemon or lime juice
watercress sprigs and cucumber slices to garnish

Preheat the oven to 250°C.

Place the chicken breasts in a shallow ovenproof dish and dot with the butter. Season with salt and pepper to taste and combination bake at 250°C using 50% (medium) microwave power for 18–20 minutes, turning over once, until cooked and light golden.

To make the sauce, place the butter in a bowl and microwave at 100% (high) microwave only for ½ minute to melt. Add the cucumber, cover and microwave at 100% (high) microwave only for 1½–2 minutes, until softened, stirring once. Add the cheese and microwave at 100% (high) microwave only for ½ minute until melted, stirring once. Mix the cornflour to a smooth paste with the milk. Add to the cheese mixture, blending well. Microwave at 100% (high) microwave only for ½–1 minute to thicken slightly. Add the nutmeg, salt and pepper and lemon or lime juice to taste. Spoon over the chicken breasts to serve.

Serve garnished with watercress sprigs and cucumber slices.

Alternative method

The above recipe can be cooked using a grill facility if your combination oven has this feature. Combination grill the chicken breasts on the wire rack for 10–12 minutes using 100% (high) microwave power.

Chicken and pepper tetrazzini

Microwave only: 100% (high)
Combination bake: 250°C using 50% (medium)
Serves: 6
Total cooking time: 24–30 minutes

175g/6oz spaghetti
1.2 litres/2 pints boiling water
1 tsp oil
175g/6oz collar bacon, rinded
40g/1½oz butter
40g/1½oz plain flour
150ml/¼ pint milk
450ml/¾ pint hot chicken stock
¼ tsp ground nutmeg
75g/3oz Cheddar cheese, grated
2 tbsp sherry
1 egg yolk
225g/8oz cooked chicken, chopped
198g/7oz can red sweet peppers, drained and sliced
25g/1oz flaked almonds

Place the spaghetti, water and oil in a bowl. Cover and microwave at 100% (high) microwave only for 10–12 minutes, or until just cooked. Leave to stand for 3 minutes, then drain.

Place the bacon on a plate, cover with absorbent kitchen towel and microwave at 100% (high) microwave only for 4–6 minutes, turning over once, until cooked and crisp. Cut into bite-sized pieces.

Place the butter in a large jug or bowl and microwave at 100% (high) microwave only for 1 minute to melt. Add the flour then gradually add the milk and stock, blending well. Microwave at 100% (high) microwave only for 4–6 minutes, stirring every 1 minute, until smooth, boiling and thickened. Add the nutmeg, cheese, sherry and egg yolk, blending well.

Preheat the oven to 250°C.

Mix the chicken with the peppers, spaghetti and bacon, blending well. Spoon into an ovenproof dish and coat with the sauce. Sprinkle with the almonds and combination bake at 250°C using 50% (medium) microwave power for 5 minutes or until heated through, golden and bubbly. Serve with a crisp green salad.

Rosy glazed crown of lamb

Microwave only: 100% (high)
Combination bake: 220°C using 50% (medium)
Serves: 6
Total cooking time: 34–41 minutes

25g/1oz butter
1 onion, peeled and chopped
2 sticks celery, scrubbed and chopped
100g/4oz streaky bacon, rinded and chopped
2 eating apples, peeled, cored and chopped
50g/2oz walnuts, chopped
2 tbsp chopped parsley
175g/6oz fresh white breadcrumbs
4 tbsp cranberry sauce
grated rind and juice of 1 lemon
salt and pepper
1 (12 rib) crown roast of lamb
Sauce and glaze:
180g/6½oz jar cranberry sauce
2 tbsp cold water
1 tsp cornflour
2 tbsp port
cutlet frills to decorate
lemon wedges and watercress sprigs to garnish

Place the butter in a bowl with the onion and celery. Cover and microwave at 100% (high) microwave only for 3 minutes, stirring once. Add the bacon and microwave at 100% (high) microwave only for a further 3 minutes, stirring twice. Add the apple, walnuts, parsley, breadcrumbs, cranberry sauce, lemon rind and juice and salt and pepper to taste, blending well. Allow to cool.

Place the crown roast in a shallow cooking dish and stuff the centre with the bacon mixture.

To make the sauce and glaze, place the cranberry sauce, water, cornflour and port in a bowl, blending well. Microwave at 100% (high) microwave only for 2–3 minutes,

stirring every 1 minute until boiling, smooth and thickened.
Use a little to brush the outside of the crown roast.

Combination bake the crown roast at 220°C using 50%
(medium) microwave power for 25–30 minutes, basting
twice with the glaze, until cooked.

To serve, top each cutlet bone with a frill. Garnish with
lemon wedges and watercress sprigs. Serve with the
remaining sauce (thinned with a little extra water or port if
liked) and reheat in the microwave at 100% (high)
microwave only for 1–2 minutes. Cut between the ribs to
serve the lamb with a little of the stuffing.

Cranberry beef Wellington

Microwave only: 100% (high)
Combination bake: 250°C using 50% (medium)
Serves: 4
Total cooking time: 23–26 minutes

1kg/2lb fillet of beef
1 garlic clove, peeled and halved
25g/1oz butter
1 onion, peeled and chopped
50g/2oz cranberry or cranberry and orange sauce
50g/2oz smooth liver pâté
1 tbsp chopped parsley
salt and pepper
370g/13oz packet frozen puff pastry, thawed
beaten egg to glaze
Cranberry wine sauce:
180g/6½oz jar cranberry sauce
6 tbsp port
1 tbsp cornflour
150ml/¼ pint water
grated rind of 1 small orange
grated rind of ½ lemon
watercress sprigs to garnish

Preheat the oven to 250°C.

Rub the fillet of beef with the cut pieces of garlic then
secure with string to a neat compact shape. Place in a

97

shallow cooking dish and combination bake at 250°C using 50% (medium) microwave power for 5 minutes. Remove from the oven and leave to cool while preparing the filling.

Finely chop the remaining garlic and place in a bowl with the butter and onion. Microwave at 100% (high) microwave only for 3 minutes, stirring once. Add the cranberry sauce, liver pâté, parsley and salt and pepper to taste, blending well.

Roll out the pastry on a lightly floured surface to a rectangle large enough to completely enclose the meat. Remove the string from the meat and place in the centre of the pastry. Cover with the cranberry mixture. Fold the pastry over, seal the edges with a little beaten egg and fold the ends underneath to make a neat package. Use any trimmings to make leaves for the top and glaze again with beaten egg. Place on a large ovenproof glass quiche or flan dish and combination bake at 250°C using 50% (medium) microwave power for 12–14 minutes, or until the pastry is richly browned, well risen and the meat is cooked medium rare. Leave to stand while making the sauce.

Place the cranberry sauce and port in a bowl and microwave at 100% (high) microwave only for 1 minute. Mix the cornflour with the water until smooth and stir into the cranberry mixture. Microwave at 100% (high) microwave only for 2–3 minutes, stirring every 1 minute, until smooth, boiling and thickened. Add the orange rind and lemon rind, blending well.

To serve, cut the cranberry beef Wellington into thick slices and serve with a little of the sauce poured over.

Beef au poivre with creamy Madeira sauce

Microwave only: 100% (high)
Combination bake: 220°C using 30% (low)
Serves: 6
Total cooking time: 31–32 minutes

1.35kg/3lb joint topside or sirloin
3 tbsp whole black peppercorns, crushed
25g/1oz butter

1 tbsp oil
5 tbsp Madeira
300ml/½ pint double cream
salt
watercress sprigs to garnish

Preheat the oven to 220°C.

Roll the joint in the peppercorns to coat evenly. Heat the
butter with the oil in a frying pan and brown the joint on
all sides. Alternatively preheat a large browning dish
according to the manufacturer's instructions, about 6
minutes at 100% (high) microwave only, add the butter and
oil and microwave at 100% (high) microwave only for ½
minute. Add the beef and turn quickly on all sides to brown
evenly.

Add the warmed Madeira, light to flame and allow the
flames to die down. Remove the meat from these juices and
place in a roasting dish. Combination bake at 220°C using
30% (low) for 30 minutes, turning twice. Leave to stand,
covered, while preparing the sauce.

Place the Madeira juices, any cooking juices from the
meat and the cream in a jug. Microwave at 100% (high)
microwave only for 1–2 minutes, stirring twice until hot and
bubbly. Season with salt to taste.

Carve the meat into thick slices onto a warmed serving
plate. Garnish with watercress sprigs and serve with the
Madeira sauce.

French cassoulet

Microwave only: 100% (high) and 50% (medium)
Combination bake: 200°C using 30% (low) and
                180°C using 30% (low)
Total cooking time: 1 hour 47 minutes–1 hour 57 minutes

450g/1lb dried haricot beans, soaked
3 garlic cloves, peeled and crushed
1 onion, peeled and sliced
350g/12oz thick cut bacon rashers, rinded
1 bouquet garni
450g/1lb belly of pork

2 duck or chicken quarter portions
175g/6oz garlic sausage, cubed
400g/14oz can chopped tomatoes
2 tbsp tomato purée
2 tsp dried Herbes de Provence
salt and pepper
75g/3oz white breadcrumbs

Place the soaked beans, garlic, onion, bacon and bouquet garni in large bowl. Cover with boiling water. Cover and microwave at 100% (high) microwave only for 12 minutes. Reduce the microwave power to 50% (medium) microwave only and cook for a further 20–25 minutes, adding extra water to cover if needed, until the beans are tender. Drain, reserving the cooking juices.

Place the pork and duck or chicken in a shallow roasting dish and combination bake at 200°C using 30% (low) for 30 minutes, turning over twice. Remove and cut into bite-sized pieces, trimming the duck or chicken from the bone.

Remove the bouquet garni from the bean mixture and discard. Add the pork, chicken or duck, garlic sausage, tomatoes, tomato purée, dried herbs and salt and pepper to taste, mixing well. Place in a deep casserole dish and pour over sufficient reserved cooking juices to three-quarters fill the dish. Sprinkle with the breadcrumbs and combination bake at 180°C using 30% (low) microwave power for 45–50 minutes, until browned and tender. Serve hot.

Bacon loin with lemon sauce

Microwave only: 100% (high)
Combination bake: 200°C using 50% (medium) then
                    180°C using 50% (medium)
Serves: 4–6
Total cooking time: 33–39 minutes

900g/2lb bacon loin joint, rinsed
½ onion, peeled and chopped
1 carrot, peeled and sliced
about 600ml/1 pint boiling water

100

Sauce:
25g/1oz butter
40g/1½oz flour
300ml/½ pint dry white wine
finely grated rind and juice of 1 lemon
4 tbsp double cream
salt and pepper

Place the bacon joint in a deep casserole dish with the onion, carrot and sufficient water to almost but not quite cover the meat. Cover and combination bake at 200°C using 50% (medium) microwave power for 15 minutes.

Turn the joint over, reduce the convection level to 180°C and combination bake at 50% (medium) microwave power for a further 15–20 minutes, or until the bacon is cooked. Leave to stand in the juices for 15 minutes.

Meanwhile, mix the butter with the flour. Place the wine, lemon rind, lemon juice, cream and salt and pepper to taste in a blender goblet. Add the flour mixture, drop by drop and liquidize or blend for 5 seconds. Place in a bowl and microwave at 100% (high) microwave only for 3–4 minutes, or until smooth and thickened, stirring every 1 minute. Serve hot with thick slices of the bacon joint.

Ideal accompaniments include roast potatoes, broad beans or cooked artichokes.

Puddings and Desserts

Woozy boozy savarin

Microwave only: 100% (high)
Combination bake: 250°C using 50% (medium)
Serves: 6
Total cooking time: 13½–15 minutes

Savarin:
6 tbsp milk
4 eggs
100g/4oz butter
225g/8oz strong plain white flour
1 sachet easy blend dried yeast
25g/1oz castor sugar
Glaze:
150g/5oz granulated sugar
200ml/7fl oz water
juice of ½ lemon
5 tbsp dark rum
Filling:
450g/1lb mixed fresh fruit salad (sliced strawberries, melon balls, stoned
   cherries, sliced kiwi and depipped grapes, for example)
whipped cream to decorate

Place the milk in a small jug and microwave at 100% (high)
microwave only for ½ minute to warm. Add the eggs,
beating well to blend. Place the butter in a bowl and
microwave at 100% (high) microwave only for 1–1½
minutes to melt. Mix the flour with the yeast and castor
sugar, blending well. Pour the egg mixture and butter into
the flour and beat well to incorporate and produce a batter
that is smooth and elastic. Pour into a well-buttered 23cm/
9in ring mould dish (1.2 litres/2 pint capacity) and cover
with oiled cling film. Leave in a warm place until the
mixture has risen to the top of the dish.

Preheat the oven to 250°C then combination bake the
savarin at 250°C using 50% (medium) microwave power
for 8 minutes. Leave to stand in the dish while making the
glaze.

Place the sugar and water in a large bowl and microwave
at 100% (high) microwave only for 4–5 minutes, stirring

twice, until the glaze is boiling and thickened slightly. Stir in the lemon juice and rum, blending well.

Turn the savarin out of its dish onto a wire rack and prick all over with a fine skewer. Set a plate under the rack to catch any glaze and spoon the warm glaze over the savarin and leave to soak in. Leave to cool completely then transfer to a serving plate.

Fill the centre of the savarin with the fruit mixture. Pipe with whirls of whipped cream and chill for at least 1 hour before serving.

Sticky apple and orange tart

Microwave only: 100% (high)
Combination bake: 250°C using 50% (medium)
Serves: 6–8
Total cooking time: 20–24 minutes

Crisp almond pastry:
175g/6oz plain flour
25g/1oz ground almonds
25g/1oz castor sugar
1 egg
100g/4oz butter or margarine
Filling:
675g/1½lb cooking apples, peeled, cored and thickly sliced
3 tbsp sugar
25g/1oz butter or margarine
Topping:
2 oranges, peeled, pith removed and thinly sliced
2 tbsp water
75g/3oz apricot jam or sweet orange marmalade

Sift the flour into a bowl. Make a well in the centre, add the almonds, sugar, egg and butter or margarine. Knead the mixture to a soft and pliable dough using the fingertips. Wrap in cling film and chill thoroughly for 30 minutes.

Roll out the pastry, on a lightly floured surface to a round large enough to line the base and sides of a 23cm/9in flan dish. Prick the base and chill again for 15 minutes.

Line the flan with greaseproof paper and baking beans

for baking 'blind'. Combination bake at 250°C using 50% (medium) microwave power for 5 minutes. Remove the paper and beans and fill with the apple slices overlapping the slices evenly in two layers and sprinkling with the sugar. Dot evenly with the butter or margarine and continue to combination bake at 250°C using 50% (medium) microwave power for 12–15 minutes until the apples are cooked and the pastry is crisp and golden.

Place the oranges in a bowl with the water, cover and microwave at 100% (high) microwave only for 2 minutes until lightly softened. Remove with a slotted spoon and arrange over the top of the tart. Add the jam or marmalade to the orange juices, blending well. Microwave at 100% (high) microwave only for 1–2 minutes until very hot, bubbly and thickened. Spoon or brush over the oranges to coat.

Serve warm or cold with whipped cream or clotted cream.

Baked almond and lemon continental cheesecake

Combination bake: 180°C using 50% (medium)
Serves: 6–8
Total cooking time: 27 minutes

Pastry:
50g/2oz self-raising flour
50g/2oz ground almonds
40g/1½oz unsalted butter
2 tbsp icing sugar
1 egg yolk
Filling:
225g/8oz full fat cream cheese
75g/3oz castor sugar
finely grated rind of 1 lemon
40g/1½oz chopped mixed peel
1 tbsp raisins
1 tbsp brandy
50g/2oz self-raising flour
25g/1oz ground almonds
2 large eggs, beaten
1 egg yolk
icing sugar to dust

To make the pastry, sift the flour into a bowl. Make a well in the centre, add the almonds, butter, icing sugar and egg yolk. Knead the mixture to a soft and pliable dough. Wrap in cling film and chill for 10 minutes.

Preheat the oven to 180°C.

Line the base of an 18cm/7in greased, deep round dish with a disc of greaseproof paper (if liked, place a strip of paper underneath this, extending over the sides of the dish, so that it will be easy to lift the cooked cheesecake from the dish once cooked). Roll out the pastry, on a lightly floured surface, to about an 18cm/7in round. Press into the base of the prepared dish, taking care since the pastry is very fragile. Combination bake at 180°C using 50% (medium) microwave power for 2 minutes.

Meanwhile, beat the cream cheese with the sugar and lemon rind. Fold in the mixed peel, raisins, brandy, flour, almonds. eggs and egg yolk, blending well. Pour over the pastry base and combination bake at 180°C using 50% (medium) microwave power for a further 25 minutes, or until puffed up, firm to the touch and golden brown. Remove from the oven but leave to cool in the dish – the filling will sink slightly on cooling.

To serve. remove the cheesecake from the dish by loosening the edges with a sharp knife and lifting out via the greaseproof paper handles. Place on a serving plate and dust liberally with icing sugar. Serve fresh with a fruit sauce made of finely chopped fruits like banana, strawberry and apricots or plain with fromage blanc or single cream.

Festive mincemeat tart

Combination bake: 220°C using 50% (medium)
Serves: 6–8
Total cooking time: 10–12 minutes

250g/9oz shortcrust pastry (made with 250g plain flour. 125g/4½oz butter
  or margarine and 4 tbsp water)
450g/1lb mincemeat
2 tbsp brandy or curaçao

grated rind of 1 orange
75g/3oz seedless green grapes
icing sugar to dust

Preheat the oven to 220°C.

Roll out two-thirds of the prepared pastry, on a lightly
floured surface, to a round large enough to line the base
and sides of a 20cm/8in flan dish.

Mix the mincemeat with the brandy or curaçao, orange
rind and grapes, blending well. Spoon evenly into the flan
case. Roll out the remaining pastry and cut into narrow
strips, about 1cm/½in wide. Arrange half the strips at
regular intervals across the filling one way then place the
remaining strips at right angles to the first. Trim the ends
and dampen with a little water to seal to the pastry rim.
Alternatively make an interwoven lattice by folding back
alternate strips of the first lattice of strips and add the second
batch of strips at right angles. Replace the folded back
strips and lift back across the alternate ones and continue
until complete.

Combination bake at 220°C using 50% (medium)
microwave power for 10–12 minutes or until the pastry is
crisp and golden. Serve warm or cold dusted with sifted
icing sugar with custard or cream.

Tia Maria and chocolate soufflé

Microwave only: 100% (high)
Combination bake: 200°C using 100% (high)
Serves: 4–6
Total cooking time: 13½–16½ minutes

75g/3oz butter
50g/2oz plain flour
250ml/8fl oz milk
50ml/2fl oz Tia Maria liqueur
100g/4oz plain chocolate, grated
4 eggs separated
50g/2oz castor sugar
2 tbsp icing sugar, sifted
single cream to serve

Place the butter in a large bowl and microwave at 100% (high) microwave only for 1½ minutes to melt. Add the flour and milk, blending well. Microwave at 100% (high) microwave only for 3–4 minutes, until boiling, thickened and smooth, stirring every 1 minute.

Add the Tia Maria and chocolate and microwave at 100% (high) microwave only for a further 1 minute, stirring once.

Preheat the oven to 200°C.

Blend the egg yolks and castor sugar into the sauce, beating well. Whisk the egg whites until they stand in stiff peaks. Fold into the chocolate mixture with a metal spoon. Turn into a greased 1.5 litre/2½ pint soufflé dish.

Combination bake at 200°C using 100% (high) microwave power for 8–10 minutes, until well risen and just firm to the touch. Serve at once dusted with the icing sugar.

Serve with lashings of single cream.

Nursery style treacle tart

Microwave only: 100% (high)
Combination bake: 200°C using 30% (low)
Serves: 6
Total cooking time: 21 minutes

Rich shortcrust pastry:
175g/6oz plain flour
pinch of salt
100g/4oz butter
2–3 tsp cold water
Filling:
450g/1lb golden syrup
2 tsp grated lemon rind
25g/1oz butter
4 tbsp single cream
2 eggs, beaten
50g/2oz breadcrumbs
whipped cream to decorate

Prepare the pastry by sifting the flour and salt into a bowl. Add the butter and cut into the flour with a knife. Rub in with the fingertips until the mixture resembles fine breadcrumbs. Sprinkle the water over the crumbs and mix to form a firm dough. Roll out on a lightly floured surface to form a round large enough to line a 20cm/8in flan dish.

Place the syrup in a bowl and microwave at 100% (high) microwave only for 1 minute. Add the lemon rind, butter, cream, eggs and breadcrumbs, blending well to ensure the butter melts.

Preheat the oven to 200°C.

Spoon the filling into the tart and combination bake at 200°C using 30% (low) microwave power for 20 minutes, or until the pastry is crisp and cooked and the filling is set.

Serve hot or cold, decorated with whipped cream.

Honey bread and butter pudding

Microwave only: 100% (high)
Combination bake: 220°C using 50% (medium)
Serves: 4–6
Total cooking time: 17 minutes

4 large slices bread, crusts removed
25g/1oz butter
6 tbsp set honey
25g/1oz sultanas, soaked in a little water to plump
225ml/8fl oz single cream
225ml/8oz milk
few drops of vanilla essence
2 eggs, beaten
½ tsp lemon juice

Spread the bread slices with the butter and some of the honey. Cut each slice into quarters and arrange in a buttered 1 litre/1¾ pint dish. Drain the sultanas and sprinkle over the bread mixture.

Place the cream and milk in a jug and microwave at 100% (high) microwave only for 2 minutes. Stir in the vanilla essence, blending well. Beat in the eggs and lemon juice then gradually pour over the bread mixture and leave to soak for 20 minutes.

Combination bake at 220°C using 50% (medium) microwave power for 15 minutes until golden and lightly set. Serve warm.

St Clement's saucy pudding

Combination bake: 220°C using 50% (medium)
Serves: 4
Total cooking time: 8–10 minutes

100g/4oz butter or margarine
100g/4oz castor sugar
grated rind of 1 lemon
grated rind of 1 small orange
3 tbsp lemon juice
3 tbsp orange juice
2 eggs, separated
75g/3oz self-raising flour
250ml/8fl oz milk

Preheat the oven to 220°C.

Cream the butter or margarine with the sugar until light and fluffy. Beat in the lemon rind, orange rind, lemon juice, orange juice and egg yolks, blending well. Gradually mix in the flour and milk to make a smooth mixture. Whisk the egg whites until they stand in stiff peaks and fold into the citrus mixture with a metal spoon.

Spoon into a well greased 23cm/9in deep pie dish or ovenproof dish and combination bake at 220°C using 50% (medium) microwave power for 8–10 minutes, or until the pudding is well risen, golden and cooked. When cooked the pudding separates into a delicious golden sponge topped crown with underneath a gooey citrus sauce.

Red cherry wine clafoutis

Combination bake: 250°C using 50% (medium)
Serves: 4–6
Total cooking time: 14–15 minutes

450g/1lb red cherries, stoned
100g/4oz castor sugar
100g/4oz plain flour
2 eggs, beaten
300ml/½ pint milk
1 tbsp cherry brandy
25g/1oz butter
castor sugar to sprinkle

Place the cherries in a well buttered 1 litre/1¾ pint shallow ovenproof dish and sprinkle with half of the sugar (use a little less sugar if the cherries are very sweet).

Preheat the oven to 250°C.

Sift the flour into a bowl, make a well in the centre and add the eggs and milk. Gradually work the flour into the eggs and milk and beat to make a smooth batter. Stir in the remaining sugar and cherry brandy. Pour over the cherries evenly.

Dot with the butter and combination bake at 250°C using 50% (medium) microwave power for 14–15 minutes or until well risen and firm to the touch.

Sprinkle with castor sugar and serve warm with cream.

Variation:

Golden sherried clafoutis

Prepare and cook as above but use golden yellow halved and stoned plums instead of cherries and sweet sherry instead of cherry brandy.

Apple and pear pie

Combination bake: 220°C using 50% (medium)
Serves: 4–6
Total cooking time: 15 minutes

350g/12oz cooking apples, peeled, cored and sliced
350g/12oz cooking pears, peeled, cored and sliced
100g/4oz soft light brown sugar
2 tbsp cornflour

175g/6oz shortcrust pastry (made with 175g/6oz plain flour, 75g/3oz butter or margarine and 2–3 tbsp water)
beaten egg to glaze
castor sugar to dust

Mix the apples with the pears, sugar and cornflour and use to fill a medium sized pie dish.

Preheat the oven to 220°C.

Roll out the prepared pastry, on a lightly floured surface, to an oval or round about 4cm/1½in larger than the pie dish, and trim a 2.5cm/1in strip from the edge of the pastry to make a pastry collar. Moisten the pie dish rim with water and press the pastry collar firmly onto the rim, overlapping the ends. Dampen the pastry collar with water then top with the pastry lid and press firmly together. Trim away any excess pastry with a knife and knock up the crust to seal. Flute the edges of the pie decoratively and decorate with any pastry trimmings if liked. Glaze with beaten egg and sprinkle with castor sugar.

Combination bake at 220°C using 50% (medium) microwave power for 15 minutes, or until well risen, golden brown and cooked through. Serve hot or cold with whipped cream.

Variations:

Rhubarb and ginger pie

Prepare and cook as above using 675g/1½lb sliced rhubarb and 15g/½oz chopped preserved ginger instead of the apples and pears.

Plum and orange pie

Prepare and cook as above using 675g/1½lb halved and stoned plums with the grated rind of 1 small orange instead of the apples and pears.

Microwave only fresh and frozen fruit cooking guide

Apples

POACHED IN LIGHT SYRUP   Peel, core and slice apples and place in a cooking dish with 300ml/½ pint hot sugar-syrup. Cover loosely and cook for the time specified, stirring once. Leave to stand, covered, for 5 minutes. Serve hot or cold.

Quantity	Power	Minutes
450g/1lb	100% (high)	3
900g/2lb	100% (high)	5–6

STEWED   Peel, core and slice apples and place in a cooking dish with sugar. Cover loosely and cook for the time specified, stirring once. Serve hot or cold.

Quantity	Sugar	Power	Minutes
450g/1lb	100g/4oz	100% (high)	6–8

BAKED   Wash and remove the cores from the apples and, using a sharp knife, score a cut around the middle of each to prevent bursting. Place in a cooking dish and add a little sugar, dried fruit and butter to each if preferred. Pour water around fruit and cook for time specified, rearranging once.

Quantity	Water	Power	Minutes
4 large	8 tbsp	100% (high)	9–10

FROZEN DRY-PACK APPLE SLICES   Place in a dish, cover and cook for the time specified, stirring once. Leave to stand, covered, for 5 minutes before using.

Quantity	Power	Minutes
450g/1lb	100% (high)	4–8

FROZEN SYRUP-SOAKED AND PACKED APPLE SLICES   Place in a dish, cover and cook for the time specified, stirring once. Leave to stand, covered, for 5 minutes before using.

113

Quantity	Power	Minutes
450g/1lb	100% (high)	8–12

FROZEN FREE-FLOW APPLE SLICES   Place in a dish, cover and cook for the time specified, stirring once. Leave to stand, covered, for 5 minutes before using.

Quantity	Power	Minutes
225g/8oz	20% (defrost)	3–4
450g/1lb	20% (defrost)	8

FROZEN APPLE PURÉE   Place in a dish, cover and cook for the time specified, breaking up and stirring 2–3 times. Leave to stand, covered, for 5 minutes before using.

Quantity	Power	Minutes
300ml/½ pint	20% (defrost)	5–7
600ml/1 pint	20% (defrost)	10–12

Apricots

POACHED IN LIGHT SYRUP   Skin, halve and stone, slicing if preferred. Place in a cooking dish with 300ml/½ pint hot sugar-syrup. Cover loosely and cook for the time specified, stirring once. Leave to stand, covered, for 5 minutes. Serve hot or cold.

Quantity	Power	Minutes
6–8	100% (high)	3–4

TO STEW FRESH   Stone and wash apricots. Place in a cooking dish, sprinkle with the sugar, cover and cook for the time specified, stirring once. Leave to stand, covered, for 5 minutes before serving.

Quantity	Sugar	Power	Minutes
6–8	100g/4oz	100% (high)	6–8

FROZEN HALVES   Place in a dish, cover and cook for the time specified, separating once. Leave to stand, covered, for 10–15 minutes before using.

114

Quantity	Power	Minutes
225g/8oz	20% (defrost)	4–5
450g/1lb	20% (defrost)	7–9

FROZEN HALVES IN SYRUP Place in a dish, cover and cook for the time specified, breaking up and stirring twice. Leave to stand, covered, for 10 minutes before using.

Quantity	Power	Minutes
225g/8oz	20% (defrost)	10–12
450g/1lb	20% (defrost)	13–15

Bananas

TO BAKE Peel and halve the bananas lengthwise. Place in a cooking dish with a little sugar and fruit juice. Cook for the time specified, stirring or rearranging twice.

Quantity	Power	Minutes
2 large	100% (high)	3–4

Blackberries

POACHED IN LIGHT SYRUP Hull and rinse. Place in a cooking dish with 300ml/½ pint hot sugar-syrup. Cover loosely and cook for the time specified, stirring once. Leave to stand, covered, for 5 minutes. Serve hot or cold.

Quantity	Power	Minutes
450g/1lb	100% (high)	2

FROZEN To thaw, place in a dish and cook for the time specified, stirring once to loosen and rearrange.

Quantity	Power	Minutes
225g/8oz	20% (defrost)	3–5

Blackcurrants

FRESH Top and tail and place in a cooking dish with the sugar and water. Cover loosely and cook for the time specified, stirring once. Leave to stand for 5 minutes before serving.

Quantity	Sugar	Water	Power	Minutes
450g/1lb	100g/4oz	2 tbsp	100% (high)	5

FROZEN   Place in a cooking dish with the sugar and water. Cover loosely and cook for the time specified, stirring once. Leave to stand for 5 minutes before serving.

Quantity	Sugar	Water	Power	Minutes
450g/1lb	100g/4oz	2 tbsp	100% (high)	4–6

Cherries

POACHED IN LIGHT SYRUP   Prick and stone if preferred. Place in a cooking dish with 300ml/½ pint hot sugar-syrup. Cover loosely and cook for the time specified, stirring once. Leave to stand, covered, for 5 minutes. Serve hot or cold.

Quantity	Power	Minutes
450g/1lb	100% (high)	2–3

STEWED   Stone, wash and place in a cooking dish with the sugar and a little grated lemon rind if preferred. Cover and cook for the time specified, stirring once. Leave to stand, covered, for 3–5 minutes before serving.

Quantity	Sugar	Power	Minutes
450g/1lb	100g/4oz	100% (high)	4–5

FROZEN   Place in a dish, cover and cook for the time specified, stirring once. Leave to stand, covered, for 5 minutes before using.

Quantity	Power	Minutes
225g/8oz	20% (defrost)	4–5
450g/1lb	20% (defrost)	6–8

Cranberries

FROZEN   To thaw, place in a shallow dish and cook for the time specified, stirring once every minute. Use as required.

116

Quantity	Power	Minutes
175g/6oz	20% (defrost)	3–4

Damsons

POACHED IN LIGHT SYRUP   Prick whole damsons or halve and stone them. Place in a cooking dish with 300ml/½ pint hot sugar-syrup. Cover loosely and cook for the time specified, stirring once. Leave to stand, covered, for 5 minutes. Serve hot or cold.

Quantity	Power	Minutes
450g/1lb whole	100% (high)	3
450g/1lb halved	100% (high)	2

STEWED   Stone and wash. Place in a cooking dish with the sugar and a little grated lemon rind if desired. Cover and cook for the time specified, stirring once. Leave to stand, covered, for 3–5 minutes before serving.

Quantity	Sugar	Power	Minutes
450g/1lb	100g/4oz	100% (high)	4–5

FROZEN WHOLE   Place in a cooking dish. Cover and cook for the time specified, stirring once. Leave to stand, covered, for 5–10 minutes before using.

Quantity	Power	Minutes
225g/8oz	20% (defrost)	4–5
450g/1lb	20% (defrost)	7–8

Gooseberries

FRESH   Top and tail and place in a cooking dish with the water. Cover and cook for the time specified. Stir in the sugar and leave to stand, covered, for 5 minutes.

Quantity	Water	Sugar	Power	Minutes
450g/1lb	2 tbsp	100g/4oz	100% (high)	4–6

FROZEN   To thaw, place in a dish and cook for the time
specified, stirring once. Leave to stand for 5 minutes.

Quantity	Power	Minutes
450g/1lb	20% (defrost)	8–10

Grapefruit

TO SERVE HOT   Cut grapefruit in half and, using a knife,
loosen the segments. Top with a little sugar and spice and
a cherry if preferred. Place in a dish and cook, uncovered,
for the time specified, rotating the dish twice. Serve at once.

Quantity	Power	Minutes
2 whole, halved	100% (high)	3

FROZEN SEGMENTS IN SYRUP   Place in a dish, cover and cook
for the time specified, separating the fruit as it thaws. Leave
to stand, covered, for 10 minutes before serving.

Quantity	Power	Minutes
225g/8oz	20% (defrost)	7–8
450g/1lb	20% (defrost)	9–12

Grapes

FROZEN SEEDLESS IN SYRUP   Place in a dish, cover and cook
for the time specified, separating the fruit as it thaws. Leave
to stand, covered, for 5–10 minutes before serving.

Quantity	Power	Minutes
225g/8oz	20% (defrost)	4–5
450g/1lb	20% (defrost)	8–10

Melon

FROZEN IN SYRUP   Place in a dish, cover and cook for the
time specified, separating the fruit as it thaws. Leave to
stand, covered, for 5–10 minutes before serving.

Quantity	Power	Minutes
225g/8oz	20% (defrost)	6
450g/1lb	20% (defrost)	12

Nectarines

POACHED IN LIGHT SYRUP Skin and prick thoroughly. Place in a cooking dish with 300ml/½ pint hot sugar-syrup and a dash of lemon juice. Cover loosely and cook for the time specified, stirring once. Leave to stand, covered, for 5 minutes. Serve hot or cold.

Quantity	Power	Minutes
8	100% (high)	6

TO STEW SLICES Stone, wash and slice. Place in a dish with the sugar. Cover and cook for the time specified, stirring once. Leave to stand, covered, for 5 minutes before serving.

Quantity	Sugar	Power	Minutes
4 medium	100g/4oz	100% (high)	4–5

FROZEN HALVES IN SYRUP Place in a dish, cover and cook for the time specified, breaking up after half the time. Leave to stand, covered, for 10 minutes before using.

Quantity	Power	Minutes
225g/8oz	20% (defrost)	10–12
450g/1lb	20% (defrost)	13–15

FROZEN SLICES IN SYRUP Place in a dish, cover and cook for the time specified, stirring once. Leave to stand, covered, for 5 minutes before using.

Quantity	Power	Minutes
225g/8oz	20% (defrost)	6–7
450g/1lb	20% (defrost)	12–13

Oranges

POACHED IN LIGHT SYRUP Peel if preferred, or scrub the skin, then finely slice. Place in a cooking dish with 300ml/

½ pint hot sugar-syrup. Cover loosely and cook for the time specified, stirring once. Leave to stand, covered, for 5 minutes. Serve hot or cold.

Quantity	Power	Minutes
4	100% (high)	3

Peaches

POACHED IN LIGHT SYRUP   Skin, stone and slice, or skin and prick thoroughly but leave whole. Place in a cooking dish with 300ml/½ pint hot sugar-syrup. Cover loosely and cook for the time specified, stirring once. Leave to stand, covered, for 5 minutes. Serve hot or cold.

Quantity	Power	Minutes
4 whole	100% (high)	4
4 sliced	100% (high)	3

TO STEW SLICES   Stone, wash and slice. Place in a dish with the sugar. Cover and cook for the time specified, stirring once. Leave to stand, covered, for 5 minutes before serving.

Quantity	Sugar	Power	Minutes
4 medium	100g/4oz	100% (high)	4–5

FROZEN HALVES IN SYRUP   Place in a dish, cover and cook for time specified, breaking up after half the time. Leave to stand, covered, for 10 minutes before using.

Quantity	Power	Minutes
225g/8oz	20% (defrost)	10–12
450g/1lb	20% (defrost)	13–15

FROZEN SLICES IN SYRUP   Place in a dish, cover and cook for the time specified, stirring once. Leave to stand, covered, for 5 minutes before using.

Quantity	Power	Minutes
225g/8oz	20% (defrost)	6–7
450g/1lb	20% (defrost)	12–13

Pears

POACHED IN LIGHT SYRUP   Peel and prick if kept whole, or
halve and core. Place in a cooking dish with 300ml/½ pint
hot sugar-syrup. Cover loosely and cook for the time
specified, stirring once. Leave to stand, covered, for 5
minutes. Serve hot or cold.

Quantity	Power	Minutes
900g/2lb whole dessert	100% (high)	5
900g/2lb whole cooking	100% (high)	10
900g/2lb halved dessert	100% (high)	3

STEWED   Peel, halve and core. Dissolve the sugar in a little
water and pour over the pears. Cover loosely and cook for
the time specified, stirring once. Leave to stand, covered,
for 5 minutes before serving.

Quantity	Sugar	Power	Minutes
6 medium	75g/3oz	100% (high)	8–10

FROZEN HALVES IN SYRUP   Place in a cooking dish, cover
and cook for the time specified, separating pears at the end
of the cooking time. Leave to stand, covered, for 5–10
minutes before using.

Quantity	Power	Minutes
225g/8oz	20% (defrost)	11–13
450g/1lb	20% (defrost)	18–20

Pineapple

POACHED IN LIGHT SYRUP   Peel, core and cut into bite-sized
pieces. Place in a cooking dish with 300ml/½ pint hot
sugar-syrup. Cover loosely and cook for the time specified,
stirring once. Leave to stand, covered, for 5 minutes. Serve
hot or cold.

Quantity	Power	Minutes
900g/2lb	100% (high)	5

Plums

POACHED IN LIGHT SYRUP   Prick whole, or halve and stone.
Place in a cooking dish with 300ml/½ pint hot sugar-
syrup. Cover loosely and cook for the time specified, stirring
once. Leave to stand, covered, for 5 minutes. Serve hot or
cold.

Quantity	Power	Minutes
450g/1lb whole	100% (high)	3
450g/1lb halved	100% (high)	2

STEWED   Stone and wash. Place in a cooking dish with the
sugar and a little grated lemon rind if preferred. Cover and
cook for the time specified, stirring once. Leave to stand,
covered, for 3–5 minutes before serving.

Quantity	Sugar	Power	Minutes
450g/1lb	100g/4oz	100% (high)	4–5

FROZEN WHOLE   Place in a cooking dish. Cover and cook
for the time specified, stirring once. Leave to stand,
covered, for 10 minutes before using.

Quantity	Power	Minutes
225g/8oz	20% (defrost)	5–6
450g/1lb	20% (defrost)	8–9

FROZEN IN SYRUP   Place in a cooking dish. Cover and cook
for the time specified, separating the plums at the end of
the cooking time. Leave to stand, covered, for 10 minutes
before using.

Quantity	Power	Minutes
225g/8oz	20% (defrost)	5–7
450g/1lb	20% (defrost)	13–14

Raspberries

POACHED IN LIGHT SYRUP   Hull and rinse. Place in a cooking
dish with 300ml/½ pint hot sugar-syrup. Cover loosely
and cook for the time specified, stirring once. Leave to stand,
covered, for 5 minutes. Serve hot or cold.

Quantity	Power	Minutes
450g/1lb	100% (high)	2

FROZEN   To thaw, place in a dish and cook for the time
specified, stirring once to loosen and rearrange.

Quantity	Power	Minutes
225g/8oz	20% (defrost)	3–4

Redcurrants

FRESH   Top and tail and place in a cooking dish with the
sugar and water. Cover loosely and cook for the time
specified, stirring once. Leave to stand for 5 minutes before
serving.

Quantity	Sugar	Water	Power	Minutes
450g/1lb	100g/4oz	2 tbsp	100% (high)	5

FROZEN   Place in a cooking dish with the sugar and water.
Cover loosely and cook for the time specified, stirring once.
Leave to stand for 5 minutes before serving.

Quantity	Sugar	Water	Power	Minutes
450g/1lb	100g/4oz	2 tbsp	100% (high)	4–6

Rhubarb

FRESH   Cut into 2.5cm/1in lengths. Place in a cooking dish
with the water. Cover loosely and cook for the time
specified, stirring once. Stir in the sugar and lemon juice.
Leave to stand, covered, for 2–3 minutes.

123

Quantity	Water	Sugar	Lemon juice	Power	Minutes
350g/12oz	2 tbsp	100g/4oz	1 tsp	100% (high)	6–7

POACHED IN LIGHT SYRUP   Cut into 2.5cm/1in lengths. Place in a cooking dish with 300ml/½ pint hot sugar-syrup. Cover loosely and cook for the time specified, stirring once. Leave to stand, covered, for 5 minutes. Serve hot or cold.

Quantity	Power	Minutes
450g/1lb	100% (high)	4

FROZEN PIECES   Place in a cooking dish, cover and cook for the time specified, stirring once. Leave to stand, covered, for 5–10 minutes before using.

Quantity	Power	Minutes
225g/8oz	20% (defrost)	5–6
450g/1lb	20% (defrost)	8–9

Strawberries

POACHED IN LIGHT SYRUP   Hull and rinse. Place in a cooking dish with 300ml/½ pint hot sugar-syrup. Cover loosely and cook for the time specified, stirring once. Leave to stand, covered, for 5 minutes. Serve warm or cold.

Quantity	Power	Minutes
450g/1lb	100% (high)	2

FROZEN   To thaw, place in a dish, cover and cook for the time specified, stirring gently twice. Leave to stand for 5–10 minutes before using.

Quantity	Power	Minutes
225g/8oz	20% (defrost)	4–5
450g/1lb	20% (defrost)	6–7

124

Home baking

Savoury

Sweet

Basic white bread

Combination bake: 220°C using 30% (low)
Makes: 3 small loaves
Total cooking time: 15–20 minutes plus proving time

675g/1½lb strong plain white flour
1 tsp salt
50g/2oz butter or margarine
1 sachet easy blend dried yeast
400ml/14fl oz warm water or water and milk mixed
beaten egg to glaze
nibbed wheat to sprinkle (optional)

Sift the flour and salt into a bowl. Rub in the butter or margarine and stir in the yeast. Add the liquid and mix to a smooth dough. Turn out onto a lightly floured surface and knead until smooth and elastic, about 5–10 minutes. Place in an oiled bowl and leave to rise until doubled in size.

Turn the dough onto a lightly floured surface, knock back to release all the air bubbles and knead again for 5 minutes. Divide the dough into three equal pieces and shape each to fit three small greased loaf dishes. Place in the dishes, cover with cling film and leave to rise until doubled in size. Glaze with beaten egg and sprinkle with nibbed wheat if liked.

Preheat the oven to 220°C.

Place the loaves on a baking tray suitable for your oven or place on the turntable. Combination bake at 220°C using 30% (low) microwave power for 15–20 minutes, or until well risen, golden and cooked. When they are cooked the loaves should sound hollow when rapped on the bottom with the knuckles. Allow to cool on a wire rack.

Granary and wholemeal bread

Combination bake: 220°C using 30% (low)
Makes: 3 small loaves
Total cooking time: 15–20 minutes

350g/12oz plain wholemeal flour
350g/12oz granary flour

1 tsp salt
25g/1oz butter or margarine
25g/1oz lard
1 sachet easy blend dried yeast
400ml/14fl oz warm water or water and milk mixed
cracked wheat to sprinkle

Sift the flours and salt into a bowl, adding any bran left in the sieve. Rub in the fats and stir in the yeast. Add the liquid and mix to a smooth dough. Turn out onto a lightly floured surface and knead until smooth and elastic, about 5–10 minutes. Place in an oiled bowl and leave to rise until doubled in size.

Turn the dough onto a lightly floured surface, knock back to release all the air bubbles and knead again for 5 minutes. Divide the dough into three equal pieces and shape each to fit three small greased loaf dishes. Place in the dishes, cover with cling film and leave to rise until doubled in size. Brush with a little water and sprinkle with cracked wheat.

Preheat the oven to 220°C.

Place the loaves on a baking tray suitable for your oven or place on the turntable. Combination bake at 220°C using 30% (low) microwave power for 15–20 minutes, or until well risen, golden and cooked. When they are cooked the loaves should sound hollow when rapped on the bottom with the knuckles. Allow to cool on a wire rack.

Bacon and apple roll

Microwave only: 100% (high)
Combination bake: 200°C using 50% (medium)
Serves: 4
Total cooking time: 21–23 minutes

350g/12oz middle cut bacon rashers, rinded and chopped
1 large onion, peeled and chopped
1 large cooking apple, peeled, cored and grated
1 tsp soft brown sugar
salt and pepper
Pastry:
225g/8oz self-raising flour

100g/4oz shredded suet
150ml/¼ pint water
beaten egg to glaze

Place the bacon and onion in a bowl. Cover and microwave at 100% (high) microwave only for 6 minutes, stirring twice. Add the apple, sugar and pepper to taste, blending well.

Preheat the oven to 200°C.

To make the pastry, mix the flour with the suet and a pinch of salt. Stir in the water to make a soft pliable dough. Knead until smooth then roll out, on a lightly floured surface, to a rectangle measuring 25 × 20cm/10 × 8in. Spread the filling over the pastry, almost to the edges. Roll up the pastry from the shortest end like a Swiss roll and seal the edges to enclose the filling.

Place, seam side down, on a large flan dish or ovenproof plate and glaze with beaten egg. Combination bake at 200°C using 50% (medium) microwave power for 15–17 minutes, or until the pastry is well risen, golden brown and the filling is cooked. Serve hot cut into thick slices.

Creamy tuna and sesame braid

Combination bake: 250°C using 50% (medium)
Serves: 6
Total cooking time: 12–15 minutes

2 × 198g/7oz cans tuna in brine, drained and flaked
2 sticks celery, scrubbed and finely sliced
½ red pepper, cored, seeded and chopped
3 tbsp garlic and chive mayonnaise
salt and pepper
Pastry:
225g/8oz plain flour
100g/4oz butter or margarine
3–4 tbsp water
2 tbsp sesame seeds
beaten egg to glaze

Preheat the oven to 250°C. Mix the tuna with the celery,

red pepper, garlic and chive mayonnaise and salt and
pepper to taste, blending well.

To make the pastry, sift the flour into a bowl. Rub in the
butter or margarine until the mixture resembles fine
breadcrumbs. Stir in half of the sesame seeds and sufficient
water to bind to a firm but pliable dough. Roll out the
pastry, on a lightly floured surface, to a rectangle measuring
about 25 × 30cm/12 × 10in.

Spoon the tuna mixture down the centre of the pastry,
leaving a 5cm/2in-border at the short edges. Make cuts
into the pastry, from the long edges at 2.5cm/1in intervals
ready for plaiting. Brush the pastry with beaten egg and
plait over the filling by crossing alternate strips of pastry
from either side over the filling and pressing down lightly to
seal. Glaze with beaten egg and sprinkle with the remaining
sesame seeds.

Place on a large flan dish or ovenproof plate and
combination bake at 250°C using 50% (medium)
microwave power for 12–15 minutes, or until cooked and
golden. Serve hot or cold cut into slices with salad. A super
picnic dish.

Cornish pasties

Combination bake: 220°C using 50% (medium)
Serves: 4
Total cooking time: 18–20 minutes

225g/8oz minced beef
1 small potato, peeled and diced
1 onion, peeled and chopped
½ tsp dried mixed herbs
1 tbsp chopped parsley
salt and pepper
2 tbsp beef stock
225g/8oz shortcrust pastry (made with 225g/8oz plain flour, 100g/4oz
  butter or margarine and 4 tbsp cold water)
beaten egg to glaze

Mix the meat with the potato, onion, herbs, parsley, salt
and pepper to taste and stock, blending well.

Preheat the oven to 220°C.

Roll out the pastry, on a lightly floured surface, and cut out four 20cm/8in rounds. Divide the meat and vegetable mixture between the circles. Dampen the pastry edges with water and draw the rounds up to make a seam across the top. Crimp the edges and brush with beaten egg to glaze. Place equally on two ovenproof plates or shallow dishes. Place one on the turntable or base of the oven and the other on the wire rack above. Combination bake at 220°C using 50% (medium) microwave power for 12 minutes.

Exchange the pasties from the wire rack to the turntable or base of the oven and those that have been cooking on the turntable or base to the wire rack and continue to combination bake at 220°C using 50% (medium) microwave power for 6–8 minutes, or until cooked, golden and crisp. Serve warm or cold.

Sausage picnic pie

Combination bake: 220°C using 100% (high) and
                     220°C using 30% (low)
Serves: 4
Total cooking time: 15–20 minutes

250g/8¾oz packet frozen puff pastry, thawed
225g/8oz pork sausagemeat
1 small apple, peeled, cored and chopped
1 tsp dried oregano
salt and pepper
50g/2oz cream cheese
1 tbsp tomato purée or chutney
beaten egg to glaze

Divide the pastry in half and roll out each piece, on a lightly floured surface, to a 15cm/6in round.

Mix the sausagemeat with the apple, oregano and salt and pepper to taste. Form into a flat round measuring about 13cm/5in across. Mix the cheese with the tomato purée or chutney and salt and pepper to taste.

Place the sausagemeat round on top of one piece of pastry.

Spread with the cheese mixture. Brush the pastry edges with beaten egg and cover with the second pastry round, sealing the edges well and crimping decoratively. Make three deep slashes in the top with a knife, place on an ovenproof plate or flan dish and glaze with beaten egg.

Combination bake at 220°C using 100% (high) microwave power for 5 minutes. Reduce the microwave power to 30% (low) and combination bake at 220°C using 30% (low) microwave power for 10–15 minutes, or until well risen, golden and cooked.

Serve hot or cold cut into slices. A delicious pie to take on a picnic.

Danish sausage rolls

Combination bake: 250°C using 50% (medium)
Makes: 10
Total cooking time: 12–13 minutes

2 large Danish gammon steaks, trimmed and cubed
1 onion, peeled and quartered
1 tbsp chopped parsley
pepper
370g/13oz packet frozen puff pastry, thawed
beaten egg to glaze

Place the gammon, onion and parsley in a processor or blender and process until evenly chopped. Season with pepper to taste. Divide the mixture in half and roll each into a long roll, about 33cm/13in long.

Preheat the oven to 250°C.

Roll out the pastry, on a lightly floured surface, to a rectangle about 28 × 33cm/11 × 13in. Cut in two lengthwise. Place each gammon roll on the pastry pieces, dampen the edges with water and fold over the filling to completely enclose, sealing the edges firmly. Glaze with beaten egg and cut each roll into 5 pieces.

Place on two ovenproof plates or flan dishes. Place one on the turntable or base of the oven and the second on the wire rack above. Combination bake at 250°C using 50% (medium) microwave power for 10 minutes, or until the rolls on the wire rack are cooked and golden brown. Remove and allow to cool on a wire rack. Transfer the rolls from the turntable or base of the oven to the wire rack and combination bake at 250°C using 50% (medium) microwave power for a further 2–3 minutes, until cooked and golden brown. Serve warm or cold.

Victoria sponge sandwich

Combination bake: 200°C using 30% (low)
Makes: a 20cm/8in cake
Total cooking time: 15 minutes

175g/6oz butter or margarine
175g/6oz castor sugar
3 eggs, beaten
175g/6oz self-raising flour, sifted
2 tbsp milk
3–4 tbsp jam
sifted icing sugar to dust

Preheat the oven to 200°C. Grease and line the base of a 20cm/8in deep round cake dish with greaseproof paper.

Cream the butter or margarine with the sugar until light and fluffy. Beat in the eggs with a little of the flour. Carefully fold in the remaining flour. Spoon into the cake dish and smooth the surface, making a small hollow in the centre of the mixture.

Combination bake at 200°C using 30% (low) microwave power for 15 minutes, or until browned and the top springs back when lightly touched with the fingertips. Leave to stand in the dish for 5–10 minutes before turning out to cool on a wire rack.

When cool cut the cake in half and sandwich together again with the jam. Dust the top with icing sugar. Cut into wedges to serve.

Variations:

Lemon or orange victoria sponge sandwich

Prepare and cook as above but cream the butter and sugar with the finely grated rind of 1 lemon or small orange. Sandwich together with orange or lemon curd instead of the jam.

Coffee and walnut victoria sponge sandwich

Prepare and cook as above but cream the butter and sugar with 1 tablespoon coffee and chicory essence. Stir in 25g/1oz chopped walnuts with the flour, blending well. Sandwich together with whipped cream instead of the jam.

Celebration rich fruit cake

Combination bake: 140°C using 30% (low)
Makes: 1 (15cm/6in) round cake
Total cooking time: 55 minutes–1¼ hours

150g/5oz butter
150g/5oz brown sugar
grated rind of ¼ lemon
3 eggs, beaten
175g/6oz plain flour
¼ tsp ground mixed spice
¼ tsp ground cinnamon
225g/8oz currants
100g/4oz sultanas
100g/4oz raisins
50g/2oz glacé cherries, halved
25g/1oz chopped mixed peel
25g/1oz flaked almonds
1 tbsp brandy

Cream the butter with the sugar until light and fluffy. Beat in the lemon rind and eggs, a little at a time, adding a little flour if the mixture starts to curdle. Sift the flour with

the spice and cinnamon and fold into the creamed mixture.
Fold in the fruit, nuts and brandy, blending well.

Spoon into a greased and lined 15cm/6in round cake dish
or tin (if your microwave allows this). Make a slight hollow
in the centre to enable the cake to rise evenly.

Combination bake at 140°C using 30% (low) for 55
minutes–1¼ hours or until a skewer inserted into the
centre of the cake comes out clean. Allow to cool slightly
then turn out onto a wire rack to cool completely. Store
for 1 month in an airtight tin to allow the flavours to develop.

Speedy Christmas cake

Combination bake: 140°C using 30% (low)
Makes: 1 (15cm/6in) round cake
Total cooking time: 55 minutes–1¼ hours

1 (15cm/6in) cooked round celebration rich fruit cake (see page 133)
Icing:
40g/1½oz butter
175g/6oz icing sugar, sifted
1 tbsp pineapple juice
25g/1oz desiccated coconut
glacé fruits or Christmas novelties to decorate

Prepare and cook the cake according to the recipe
instructions on page 133.

To make the icing, beat the butter until soft. Gradually
work in the icing sugar, pineapple juice and coconut.
Spread over the top of the cake and decorate with glacé
fruits or Christmas novelties. Tie a ribbon or cake frill
around the sides of the cake to complete.

Easter mimosa cake

Combination bake: 200°C using 50% (medium)
Makes: 1 (18cm/7in) cake
Total cooking time: 9½–11 minutes

Cake:
175g/6oz butter
grated rind of 1 lemon
175g/6oz castor sugar
3 eggs
175g/6oz self-raising flour
2 tbsp milk
Filling:
3 tbsp lemon curd
Icing:
150g/5oz butter
275g/10oz icing sugar, sifted
1–2 tbsp lemon juice
Decoration:
crystallized violets
mimosa balls
angelica diamonds

Grease and line the bases of two 18cm/7in round sandwich cake dishes with greaseproof paper.

Preheat the oven to 200°C.

Beat the butter with the lemon rind and sugar until pale, light and fluffy. Beat the eggs a little at a time with the flour and milk to make a smooth batter with light dropping consistency. Divide the mixture evenly between the prepared dishes, levelling the surfaces. Place one on the turntable or base of the oven and one on the wire rack above.

Combination bake at 200°C using 50% (medium) microwave power for 7–8 minutes, or until the cake on the rack is well risen, golden and firm to the touch. Remove and allow to cool on a cooling rack. Transfer the cake from the turntable or base of the oven to the wire rack and cook for a further 2½–3 minutes, or until well risen, golden and firm to the touch. Cool on a wire rack. When cold, remove the greaseproof paper and sandwich together with the lemon curd.

To make the icing, beat the butter until soft. Gradually beat in the icing sugar and lemon juice to make a smooth icing with soft spreading consistency. Carefully coat the sides and top of the cake with the icing.

Decorate with crystallized violets, mimosa balls and angelica diamonds.

Madeira cake

Microwave only: 30% (low)
Combination bake: 250°C using 50% (medium)
Makes: 1 (18cm/7in) round cake
Total cooking time: 12½–15½ minutes

175g/6oz butter
175g/6oz castor sugar
finely grated zest of 1 lemon
3 eggs, beaten
225g/8oz plain flour
1½ tsp baking powder
2 tbsp milk
1 strip citron peel

Place the butter in a bowl and microwave at 30% (low) microwave only for ½ minute to soften.

Preheat the oven to 250°C.

Add the castor sugar and lemon zest to the butter and cream until light and fluffy. Beat in the eggs with a wooden spoon a little at a time, blending well. Sift the flour and baking powder into the creamed mixture, then fold in with the milk.

Spoon into a greased and greaseproof paper lined 18cm/7in round glass dish, and smooth surface. Place the strip of citron on top of the cake in the centre.

Combination bake at 250°C using 50% (medium) microwave power for 12–15 minutes, or until the cake is well risen, golden and cooked. Cool in the dish for 10 minutes then transfer to a cooling rack to cool further.

Variations:

Walnut cake

Prepare and cook as above but add 75g/3oz chopped walnuts and a little vanilla essence to the creamed mixture.

Cherry Madeira cake

Prepare and cook as above but add 175g/6oz chopped glacé cherries to the creamed mixture.

Eccles cakes

Combination bake: 250°C using 50% (medium)
Makes: 12
Total cooking time: 7 minutes

25g/1oz butter
1 tbsp castor sugar
½ egg yolk
finely grated rind of ½ lemon
¼ tsp ground mixed spice
¼ tsp ground nutmeg
60g/2½oz currants
15g/½oz chopped mixed candied peel
250g/8¾oz packet frozen puff pastry, thawed
milk to glaze
castor sugar to sprinkle

Preheat the oven to 250°C. Beat the butter with the sugar until light and fluffy. Beat in the egg yolk, lemon rind, spice and nutmeg. Fold in the currants and peel, blending well.

Roll out the pastry, on a lightly floured surface, and cut out twelve 10cm/4in rounds. Place an equal quantity of fruit mixture on each round. Dampen the pastry edges with water and, with the fingertips, draw up the edges of each round so that they meet in the centre, completely enclosing the filling. Press well together to seal. Turn each cake over and flatten slightly with a rolling pin. Make three slits in the top of each with a sharp knife.

Divide equally between two ovenproof plates or flan dishes and glaze with beaten egg. Sprinkle with castor sugar to coat. Place one plate on the turntable or base of the oven and one plate on the wire rack above. Combination bake at 250°C using 50% (medium) microwave power for 5 minutes by which time the Eccles cakes on the rack should be well risen, golden brown and cooked. Remove and allow to cool on a wire rack. Transfer the cakes on the turntable or base of the oven to the wire rack above and combination bake at 250°C using 50% (medium) microwave power for a further 2 minutes until cooked. Cool on a wire rack.

Banana and apricot loaf

Combination bake: 220°C using 50% (medium)
Makes: 1 900g/2lb loaf
Total cooking time: 12–14 minutes

100g/4oz butter or margarine
100g/4oz soft brown sugar
1½ tsp ground cinnamon
2 eggs
2 large ripe bananas, peeled and mashed
225g/8oz wholemeal self-raising flour
50g/2oz walnuts, chopped
75g/3oz no-need-to-soak dried apricots, chopped

Preheat the oven to 220°C. Line the base of a 18cm/7in deep round cake dish with greaseproof paper and then grease again.

Cream the butter with the sugar until light and fluffy. Add the cinnamon and eggs, one at a time, beating well to blend. Fold in the bananas and flour alternately. Stir in the walnuts and apricots, blending well. Spoon into the prepared dish and combination bake at 220°C using 50% (medium) microwave power, or until well risen, browned and firm to the touch. Test by inserting a wooden cocktail stick in the centre of the loaf – if the cocktail stick comes out clean the cake is cooked. Leave to stand for 5 minutes before turning out to cool on a wire rack.

Serve sliced plain or with butter.

Cranberry nut loaf

Combination bake: 220°C using 50% (medium)
Makes: 1 900g/2lb loaf

Total cooking time: 12–14 minutes

225g/8oz plain flour
1½ tsp baking powder
½ tsp bicarbonate of soda
1 tsp salt
50g/2oz butter or margarine
100g/4oz castor sugar
75g/3oz chopped walnuts
grated rind and juice of 2 oranges
1 egg
180g/6½oz jar cranberry sauce

Preheat the oven to 220°C. Line a 1kg/2lb loaf dish with greaseproof paper then grease again.

Sift the flour with the baking powder, bicarbonate of soda and salt. Rub in the butter or margarine until the mixture resembles fine breadcrumbs. Stir in the sugar and walnuts.

Whisk the orange rind, orange juice, egg and cranberry sauce together then stir into the flour mixture, blending well. Spoon into the prepared dish and combination bake at 220°C using 50% (medium) microwave power for 12–14 minutes, or until well risen, browned and springy to the touch. Test by inserting a wooden cocktail stick to see if cooked in the centre – if the cocktail stick comes out clean the cake is cooked. Leave to stand for 5 minutes before turning out to cool on a wire rack.

Store wrapped in foil for 2 days for best eating quality. Serve sliced and buttered.

Hot cross buns

Microwave only: 100% (high)
Combination bake: 220°C using 30% (low)
Makes: 12
Total cooking time: 14–17½ minutes plus proving time

450g/1lb strong plain white flour
pinch of salt
50g/2oz castor sugar
1 tsp ground mixed spice
½ tsp ground cinnamon

1 sachet easy blend dried yeast
50g/2oz butter, melted and cooled
1 egg, beaten
150ml/¼ pint warm milk
100g/4oz currants
50g/2oz chopped mixed peel
Glaze:
50g/2oz granulated sugar
3 tbsp milk

Sift the flour and salt into a bowl. Add the sugar, spices and yeast, blending well. Add the butter, egg, milk, currants and peel and mix to make a soft but manageable dough. Turn onto a lightly floured surface and knead until smooth and elastic, about 5 minutes. Cover with cling film and leave to rise until doubled in size.

Knock back the dough to release all the air bubbles then divide into 12 equal pieces and shape each into a ball. Place on a greased baking dish, cover with cling film and leave to rise for about 30 minutes or until the bun dough feels springy when pressed with a floured finger.

Preheat the oven to 220°C.

Remove the cling film, and using a sharp knife, slash a cross in the top of each bun. Combination bake at 220°C using 30% (low) microwave power for 12–15 minutes. Remove and allow to cool on a wire rack.

Place the sugar and milk in a small bowl. Microwave at 100% (high) microwave only for 2–2½ minutes, until boiling. Brush the warm hot cross buns twice with the glaze and leave to cool. Serve warm or cold with butter.

Combination grilling recipes

Tasty chicken and bacon bites

Microwave only: 100% (high)
Combination grill: grill high with 50% (medium)
Serves: 4
Total cooking time: 9–11 minutes

12 bacon rashers, rinded
100g/4oz cooked chicken, finely chopped
50g/2oz fresh breadcrumbs
½ tsp chopped parsley
salt and pepper
1 small egg, beaten
Spicy dip:
15g/½oz butter
1 small onion, peeled and finely chopped
4 tbsp tomato ketchup
1 tsp soft brown sugar
1 tbsp Worcestershire sauce
2 tsp white wine vinegar
¼ tsp mustard
1 tbsp mango chutney, chopped
lettuce leaves to serve

Lay the bacon rashers on a board. Mix the chicken with the breadcrumbs, parsley and salt and pepper to taste. Add sufficient egg to bind the mixture together. Place a little of the chicken filling onto each bacon rasher and secure with a wooden cocktail stick. Place on the grill rack and combination grill with the grill on high and 50% (medium) microwave power for 5–7 minutes, turning over once.

Place the butter and onion in a bowl. Cover and microwave at 100% (high) microwave only for 2 minutes. Add the tomato ketchup, sugar, Worcestershire sauce, vinegar, mustard, chutney and salt and pepper to taste. Microwave at 100% (high) microwave only for a further 2 minutes.

Place the cooked bites on a plate lined with lettuce leaves. Place the dip in a serving bowl and place in the centre of the bites. Serve while still warm.

Herb and honey chicken thighs

Combination grill: grill high with 100% (high)
Serves: 4
Total cooking time: 11–14 minutes

8 small chicken thighs, skinned
2 tbsp clear honey
4 tbsp dried breadcrumbs
2 tsp dried mixed herbs
1 tsp salt
¼ tsp ground black pepper
pinch of cayenne pepper

Roll the chicken pieces in the honey in a bowl. On a plate
mix the breadcrumbs with the herbs, salt, pepper and
cayenne. Roll the chicken thighs in the seasoned crumbs.
Place on the grill rack and combination grill on high using
100% (high) microwave power, for 11–14 minutes, turning
over twice, until golden and cooked through.

Serve hot with vegetables or salad in season.

Finger lickin' drumsticks

Combination grill: grill high with 100% (high)
Serves: 4
Total cooking time: 11–14 minutes

8 chicken drumsticks, skinned
seasoned flour to coat
1 egg beaten
40g/1½ oz dried breadcrumbs
40g/1½ oz finely grated cheese
½ tsp chopped mixed herbs
salt and pepper

Coat the chicken drumsticks in the flour. Dip in the beaten
egg and then into the breadcrumbs mixed with the cheese,
herbs and salt and pepper to taste.

Place on the grill rack and combination grill on high using
100% (high) microwave power, for 11–14 minutes, turning
over twice, until golden, bubbly and cooked through. Serve
hot or cold.

Crispy pork chops with cranberry and port sauce

Microwave only: 100% (high)
Combination grill: grill high with 50% (medium)
Serves: 4
Total cooking time: 16–21 minutes

4 pork loin chops, trimmed of excess fat
flour to coat
1 egg, beaten
75g/3oz dried breadcrumbs
2 tsp chopped parsley
salt and pepper
Sauce:
185g/6½oz jar cranberry sauce
2 tsp port
orange segments to garnish

Coat each chop in flour. Dip into the beaten egg then the breadcrumbs mixed with the parsley and salt and pepper to taste. Chill for 30 minutes for the breadcrumb mixture to set.

Preheat the grill to high. Place the chops on the grill rack and combination grill with the grill on high and 50% (medium) microwave power for 14–18 minutes, turning over once, until cooked and no longer pink.

Place the cranberry sauce and port in a bowl and microwave at 100% (high) microwave only for 2–3 minutes, stirring once, until hot and bubbly.

Serve the pork chops with the sauce, garnished with orange segments.

Lamb and cinnamon kebabs

Combination grill: grill high with 50% (medium)
Serves: 4
Total cooking time: 10–12 minutes

675g/1½lb lamb neck fillets, trimmed and cubed
Marinade:
175g/6oz yogurt
3 tbsp olive oil

144

3 tbsp chopped fresh mint
1 garlic clove, peeled and crushed
3 tbsp honey
pinch of ground cinnamon
salt and pepper
about 12 bay leaves
lemon slices to garnish

Place the lamb cubes in a bowl. Mix the yogurt with the oil, mint, garlic, honey, cinnamon and salt and pepper to taste. Pour over the lamb, cover and chill for 4–5 hours.

Drain the lamb from the marinade and thread onto wooden skewers with the bay leaves. Place on the grill rack and baste with the marinade. Combination grill on high using 50% (medium) microwave power for 10–12 minutes, turning over once and basting with the marinade twice.

Serve hot garnished with lemon slices.

Combination grilling guide for meat and poultry

	Meat or poultry	Grill setting	Microwave power level	Cooking time in minutes	Guidelines
Beef:	steak				
	2 × 225g/8oz	high	medium	5–9	Turn over once. Cook according to taste, rare to well done.
	4 × 225g/8oz	high	medium	10–13	Turn over once. Cook according to taste, rare to well done.
Lamb:	chops				
	2 loin or chump	high	medium	8–10	Place in a dish. Turn over once.
	4 loin or chump	high	medium	10–12	
Pork:	chops				
	2 loin, chump or sparerib	high	medium	10–12	Place in a dish. Turn over once.
	4 loin, chump or sparerib	high	medium	14–18	Cook according to thickness and size.
Chicken:	quarters				
	2 quarter portions	high	high	8–10	Place in a dish and turn twice during cooking.
	4 quarter portions	high	high	12–15	
	drumsticks & thighs				
	4 drumsticks or small thigh joints	high	high	7–8	Place in a dish, turn and rearrange twice during cooking.
	8 drumsticks or small thigh joints	high	high	11–14	
	boneless breasts				
	2 boneless breasts	high	high	5–6	Place in a dish and turn twice during cooking.
	4 boneless breasts	high	high	10–12	
Duck:	quarters				
	2 quarter portions	high	high	12–15	Place in a dish. Turn over twice during cooking, removing excess fat
		high	high	20–22	

Grilling only guide for ovens with grill facility

Item	Quantity	Grill setting	Total cooking time in minutes	Guidelines
Sausages:	450g/1lb	high	17	Turn over after 10 minutes
Bacon:	8 rashers	high	15	Turn over once
Beefburgers: (frozen)	4 × 100g/4oz	high	18	Turn over once
	4 × 50g/2oz	high	14	Turn over once
Trout:	2	high	16	Turn over once
Fish steaks:	4 × 75g/3oz	high	22	Turn over once
Fish fingers: (cooked from frozen)	10 × 25g/1oz	high	18	Turn over twice
Crumpets:	8	high	12	
Muffins:	4 split	high	11	

Complete meals and menus

Complete meals and menus

Many people enjoy continued success with cooking single recipe dishes in the microwave but stumble when it comes to cooking a whole meal. Individual components of the meal are cooked to perfection but timings go adrift and dishes are not ready for serving all at the same time. Experience with cooking complete meals does come with time but here are a few guidelines to help:

- For best results cook vegetables to be served as accompaniments before cooking the main dish whether meat, poultry, fish or made-up dish. Make timings a little shorter than indicated so that any reheating later will ensure the vegetables are cooked to perfection rather than overcooked. Cooking them after the main dish can mean dried out vegetables since the heat from the oven will have a parching effect.

- Cook cold starters and desserts well ahead and chill. If a recipe can be cooked ahead and then quickly reheated so much the better. Reheating can take place just before serving in the case of starters and while the main course is being served in the case of desserts.

- Reheat par-cooked vegetables while the main dish is standing. (Most dishes need this and will not cool too much with a 5–10 minutes standing time.) The exception is of course soufflés which have to be served straight from the oven to ready seated guests or family.

- Cook short timed hot desserts that cannot be cooked ahead while the main course is being served or after eating. (A short respite between courses is often welcomed.)

Typical family dinner or supper menu

Steak, kidney and horseradish pie
Cooked mixed vegetables

St Clemen:'s saucy pudding (see page 110)

Menu planner

- Prepare vegetables on day of serving.
- Prepare pudding on day of serving but do not cook.
- About 45 minutes before serving cook the vegetables making timings a little shorter than indicated so that they are slightly undercooked. (Quick reheating later will finish cooking to perfection.)
- Prepare and cook the pie. Reheat the vegetables and serve with the pie.
- Cook the pudding while eating if liked and serve hot after the main course.

Steak, kidney and horseradish pie

Microwave only: 50% (medium)
Combination bake: 220°C using 50% (medium)
Serves: 4
Total cooking time: 34–36 minutes

675g/1½lb good-quality steak and kidney, cut into bite-sized pieces
1 onion, peeled and chopped
2 tbsp plain flour
salt and pepper
2 tbsp horseradish mustard
175ml/6fl oz boiling beef stock
175g/6oz shortcrust pastry (made with 175g/6oz plain flour, 75g/3oz butter or margarine and 2–3 tbsp water)
beaten egg to glaze

Place the steak and kidney, onion, flour, salt and pepper to taste, mustard and stock in a medium-sized pie dish, blending well. Cover and microwave at 50% (medium) microwave only for 20 minutes, stirring three times. Leave to stand for 10–15 minutes or while making the pastry.

Preheat the oven to 220°C.

Roll out the prepared pastry, on a lightly floured surface, to an oval or round about 4cm/1½in larger than the pie dish. Trim a 2.5cm/1in strip from the edge of the pastry to make a pastry collar. Moisten the pie dish rim with water and press the pastry collar firmly onto the rim, overlapping the ends. Dampen the pastry collar with water then top with the pastry lid and press firmly together. Trim away any excess pastry with a knife and knock up the crust to seal. Flute the edges of the pie decoratively and decorate with any pastry trimmings if liked. Glaze with beaten egg.

Combination bake at 220°C using 50% (medium) microwave power for 14–16 minutes, or until the pastry is golden and crisp and the filling is cooked through. Serve hot with vegetables in season.

Sunday lunch menu

Sunday's stuffed roast chicken
Boiled new potatoes
Cauliflower cheese (see page 62)
Peas and carrots
Gravy

Apple and pear pie (see page 111)

Menu planner

- Prepare and cook the pie up to 24 hours ahead and chill.
- Prepare the stuffing for the chicken up to 24 hours ahead. Stuff the chicken and chill.
- Prepare the vegetables on the day of serving.
- About 1¼ hours before required cook the vegetables making timings a little shorter than indicated so that they are slightly undercooked. (Quick reheating later will finish cooking to perfection.)
- Cook the chicken according to the recipe instructions. Leave to stand while reheating the vegetables to serving temperature. Make a gravy from the chicken juices and serve with the chicken and vegetables.
- Reheat the pie to serve warm if liked or serve cold with cream or ice cream.

Sunday's stuffed roast chicken

Microwave only: 100% (high)
Combination bake: 220°C using 50% (medium) or
                    220°C using 30% (low)

Serves: 4–6
Total cooking time: 29–34½ minutes or
                     39–44½ minutes

25g/1oz butter
1 onion, peeled and finely chopped
175g/6oz pork or beef sausagemeat
50g/2oz fresh white breadcrumbs
1 tsp chopped mixed herbs
1 tbsp toasted almonds or hazelnuts, chopped
1 egg, beaten
1.5kg/3½lb oven-ready roasting chicken
watercress or parsley sprigs to garnish

Place the butter and onion in a bowl. Cover and microwave
at 100% (high) microwave only for 2 minutes, stirring
once. Add the sausagemeat, cover and microwave at 100%
(high) microwave only for a further 2–2½ minutes, stirring
twice to break up, until cooked. Add the breadcrumbs,
herbs, nuts and sufficient beaten egg to make a stuffing for
the chicken. Allow to cool.

Preheat the oven to 220°C.

Place the stuffing in the body cavity of the chicken and
secure firmly with wooden cocktail sticks or sew with string.
Truss the chicken into a neat shape and place in a cooking
dish. Combination bake at 220°C using 50% (medium)
microwave power for 25–30 minutes, or at 200°C using 30%
(low) microwave power for 35–40 minutes, basting twice with
any juices, or until the chicken is cooked, golden and the
juices from the thickest part of the bird, the thighs, run clear.

Serve hot garnished with parsley or watercress sprigs.

Cook ahead easy menu

Mid-winter casserole
Oven crispy jacket baked potatoes (see page 60) or boiled rice, boiled
  pasta

Baked almond and lemon continental cheesecake (see page 105)

Menu planner

- Prepare and cook the cheesecake up to 24 hours in advance and chill in the refrigerator until required.
- Prepare and cook the casserole up to 24 hours ahead and reheat in the microwave at 100% (high) microwave only for 10–12 minutes, stirring twice. Alternatively place all the casserole ingredients in a dish and leave in the refrigerator until about 1½ hours before required. Cook according to the recipe instructions. Leave to stand while cooking the potatoes or rice or pasta.
- Remove the cheesecake from the refrigerator 30 minutes before required.
- Serve the cooked casserole with the potatoes, rice or pasta. Follow with the cheesecake.

Mid-winter casserole

Combination bake: 170°C using 30% (low)
Serves: 4–6
Total cooking time: 1 hour 10–1 hour 20 minutes

675g/1½lb stewing steak, cubed
10 pickling or small onions, peeled
2 carrots, peeled and diced
1 small turnip, peeled and diced
2 sticks celery, scrubbed and sliced
1 tsp mixed dried herbs
1½ tsp wholegrain mustard
dash of Worcestershire sauce
400g/14oz can chopped tomatoes
300ml/½ pint red wine or beef stock
salt and pepper

Brown the meat conventionally in a frying pan if liked. Place in a large casserole dish with the onions, carrots, turnip, celery, herbs, mustard, Worcestershire sauce, tomatoes, wine or stock and salt and pepper to taste, blending well.

Cover and combination bake at 170°C using 30% (low)

for 1 hour 10–1 hour 20 minutes, until tender, stirring halfway through the cooking time.

Serve piping hot with potatoes, rice or pasta.

Formal dinner menu

Baked crab-stuffed avocados (see page 21)

Mushroom and ginger-stuffed lamb
Swiss rosti (see page 62)
French beans

Woozy boozy savarin (see page 103)

Menu planner

- Prepare and cook the savarin up to 24 hours ahead and chill.
- Prepare the stuffing for the lamb up to 24 hours ahead and use to stuff the lamb. Chill until required.
- Prepare the beans and rosti on the day.
- Prepare the avocados (leaving the folding in of the egg white until the last possible moment).
- About 1¼ hours before serving cook the beans and the rosti, making timings a little shorter than indicated so that they are slightly undercooked. (Quick reheating later will finish the cooking to perfection.) Fill the savarin with fresh fruit.
- Cook the lamb according to the recipe instructions. Leave to stand, covered with foil while cooking the avocados.
- Serve the avocados.
- Quickly reheat the beans and rosti (about 4–5 minutes at 100% (high) microwave only).
- Serve the lamb, beans and rosti.
- Follow with the savarin.

Mushroom and ginger-stuffed lamb

Microwave only: 100% (high)
Combination bake: 200°C using 30% (low)

154

Serves: 6–8
Total cooking time: 48 minutes

Stuffing:
1 small onion, peeled and finely chopped
225g/8oz flat mushrooms, wiped and finely chopped
1 tbsp soy sauce
50g/2oz fresh wholemeal breadcrumbs
2.5cm/1in piece root ginger, peeled and grated
1 egg, beaten
salt and pepper
1.8kg/4lb shoulder of lamb, boned (weight before being boned)
15g/½oz butter

Place the onion, mushrooms and soy sauce in a bowl. Cover and microwave at 100% (high) microwave only for 3 minutes, stirring once. Add the breadcrumbs, root ginger, egg and salt and pepper to taste. Spread the stuffing over the meat, roll up and secure into a neat shape with string.

Place in a roasting dish and dot with the butter. Season with salt and pepper to taste and combination bake at 200°C using 30% (low) for 45 minutes, turning twice. Leave to stand for 5–10 minutes before carving into slices to serve.

Serve hot with fresh vegetables in season and a gravy made from the dish juices if liked.

Easter celebration menu

Eggs en cocotte (see page 22)

Roast turkey with oaten ham stuffing
Carrots
Broccoli
Creamy mashed potato
Gravy

Easter mimosa cake (see page 134)

Menu planner

- Make the Easter mimosa cake up to 48 hours in advance, decorate and store in an airtight tin.

- Prepare the stuffing for the turkey up to 24 hours in advance. Stuff the turkey and chill.
- Prepare the carrots and broccoli on the day of serving.
- Prepare and cook the potatoes and place in a serving dish on the day of serving.
- About 1½ hours before serving cook the carrots and broccoli, making timings a little shorter than indicated so that they are slightly undercooked. (Quick reheating later will finish cooking to perfection.) Prepare the eggs en cocotte.
- Cook the turkey according to the recipe instructions. Leave to stand, covered with foil while cooking the eggs en cocotte.
- Serve the eggs and while eating reheat the vegetables – carrots, broccoli and mashed potatoes. (Place altogether in the microwave using the shelf if possible and microwave at 100% (high) microwave only for about 6 minutes.) If the vegetables have to be cooked in two stages reheat the potatoes first then the carrots and broccoli – the potatoes will retain their heat longer.
- Make a gravy with the turkey juices and serve the turkey with gravy and vegetables.
- Follow with the Easter mimosa cake for dessert.

Roast turkey with oaten ham stuffing

Combination bake: 200°C using 50% (medium) or
220°C using 30% (low)
Serves: 8–10
Total cooking time: 36–42 or 48 minutes

50g/2oz fresh breadcrumbs
2 tbsp chopped parsley
1 small onion, peeled and finely chopped
2 sticks celery, scrubbed and finely chopped
75g/3oz cooked ham, chopped
25g/1oz rolled oats
½ tsp dried thyme
salt and pepper
1 egg, beaten

2.7kg/6lb oven-ready turkey
25g/1oz butter
watercress sprigs to garnish

Mix the breadcrumbs with the parsley, onion, celery, ham, oats, thyme and salt and pepper to taste. Bind together with the beaten egg to make a stuffing. Spoon the stuffing into the neck cavity of the turkey and secure with a wooden cocktail stick or trussing needle and string. Place in a roasting dish and rub with the butter. Season with salt and pepper to taste.

Combination bake at 200°C using 50% (medium) microwave power for 36–42 minutes or at 220°C using 30% (low) for 48 minutes, turning twice during cooking and basting regularly. Leave to stand for 15 minutes before carving.

Serve hot or cold garnished with watercress sprigs.

Christmas dinner menu

Duck pâté en croute (see page 23)

Maple glazed Christmas gammon
Brussels sprouts with chestnuts or walnuts
Roast or boiled potatoes

Festive mincemeat tart (see page 106)

Speedy Christmas cake (see page 134)
Cheeseboard/celery/crackers/port

Menu planner

- Make the speedy Christmas cake up to 1 month ahead and leave to mature. Decorate about 48 hours before required and store in an airtight tin.
- Prepare and cook the pâté up to 24 hours ahead and chill until required.
- Prepare and cook the festive mincemeat tart up to 24 hours ahead and chill until required.
- Prepare the vegetables on the day of cooking.

157

- About 1¾ hours before required cook the boiled potatoes and Brussels sprouts making timings a little shorter than indicated so that they are slightly undercooked. (Quick reheating later will finish cooking to perfection.)
- Prepare and cook the gammon according to the recipe instructions. Leave to stand while serving the pâté.
- Reheat the potatoes and Brussel sprouts while eating. Prepare and cook the sauce and serve with the vegetables and gammon.
- Reheat the tart to serve warm if liked and serve.
- Follow with the cake, cheeseboard, celery, crackers and port.

Maple-glazed Christmas gammon

Microwave only: 100% (high)
Combination bake: 200°C using 50% (medium) and
                    180°C using 50% (medium)

Serves: 6–8
Total cooking time: 1 hour 7 minutes–1 hour 14 minutes

1.5–1.75kg/3½–4lb gammon joint
1 bay leaf
3 cloves
pinch of ground nutmeg or mace
200ml/7fl oz dry cider or apple juice
2 tbsp maple syrup
1 tsp Dijon mustard
Grapefruit and maple syrup sauce:
300ml/½ pint white wine
300ml/½ pint water
1 tsp cornflour
juice of ½ pink grapefruit
1 tbsp maple syrup
grated rind of ¼ grapefruit
½ tsp creamed horseradish
2 tsp chopped parsley
salt and pepper

Place the gammon in a large ovenproof bowl with the bay leaf, cloves, nutmeg or mace and cider or apple juice, so that the gammon is almost but not totally immersed in the

158

liquid. Cover and combination bake at 200°C using 50% (medium) microwave power for 40 minutes, turning over once halfway through the cooking time. Reduce the convection level to 180°C and combination bake at 50% (medium) microwave power for a further 10–15 minutes until cooked.

Remove the gammon from the liquid and strip off the rind using a sharp knife. Score the fat into a diamond pattern. Mix the maple syrup with the mustard and brush onto the fat surface. Return to the oven on a cooking dish and combination bake at 180°C using 50% (medium) for 10 minutes or until the fat is crisp and golden. Leave to stand while making the sauce.

Place the wine and water in a large jug and microwave at 100% (high) microwave only for 4–6 minutes, or until boiling. Mix the cornflour with the grapefruit juice to make a smooth paste. Add the maple syrup, grapefruit rind, horseradish, parsley and salt and pepper to taste. Stir into the wine mixture, blending well. Microwave at 100% (high) microwave only for 3 minutes, stirring every 1 minute to ensure the sauce is smooth.

Serve the gammon with the hot sauce. Delicious accompaniments include Brussels sprouts cooked with walnuts or chestnuts and roast potatoes.

Picnic menu

Bacon and chicken raised pie
Sausage picnic pie or Danish sausage rolls (see pages 130–132)
Mixed salad
French bread
Cheese, pâté, celery
Summer compôte or fresh fruit
Cranberry nut loaf (see page 138)
Chilled wine or fruit juice

Menu planner

● Prepare and cook the cranberry nut loaf up to 3 days ahead and store in an airtight tin.

- Prepare and cook the raised pie up to 48 hours in advance and chill until required.
- Prepare and cook the sausage rolls or picnic pie up to 24 hours ahead and chill until required.
- Prepare salad, bread, cheese, pâté, fruit compôte or fresh fruit and drinks on day of picnic.
- Pack picnic including cooked chilled items. If liked the sausage picnic pie or sausage rolls can be served warm if reheated quickly before the journey commences and they are wrapped in foil then newspaper to keep warm. Place shiny side of foil inside to retain heat.

Bacon and chicken raised pie

Microwave only: 100% (high)
Combination bake: 180°C using 30% (low)
Serves: 6–8
Total cooking time: 43½–44½ minutes

Pastry:
350g/12oz plain flour
½ tsp salt
150ml/¼ pint milk or milk and water mixed
75g/3oz lard
Filling:
550g/1¼lb collar bacon, rinded
1 small onion, peeled and chopped
2 tsp dried sage
ground black pepper
225g/8oz boneless chicken, cubed
beaten egg to glaze
Jellied stock:
65ml/2½fl oz chicken stock
1 tsp powdered gelatine

Sift the flour and salt into a bowl. Add the egg yolk and toss lightly in the flour. Place the milk or milk and water in a jug with the lard and microwave at 100% (high) microwave only for 3–4 minutes or until boiling. Pour at once onto the dry ingredients. Mix quickly to make a fairly soft dough. Turn on to a lightly floured surface and knead until smooth and elastic. Divide the pastry into a two-thirds and one-third portions. Roll out the larger piece to a large round that will cover the base and sides of a 13cm/5in diameter large jar or dish. Stand the jar upside down and shape the pastry over the base then mould up the sides to a height of about 10cm/4in. Wrap a double piece of greaseproof paper around the jar and secure with string. Cover and chill until firm. Keep the remaining pastry warm. When set, turn the jar upright and carefully ease the pastry shell away from the jar, keeping the greaseproof paper intact.

Meanwhile, cut the lean bacon meat into small cubes and mince the remaining lean and fat meat. Mix the cubed and minced bacon with the onion, sage and pepper to taste. Press half of this mixture into the prepared pastry case. Cover with the chicken then top with the remaining bacon mixture. Brush the pastry rim with water. Roll out the remaining pastry to make a lid for the pie and position on top. Trim, seal and flute the edges. Cut a cross in the centre of the pie and fold back the pieces of pastry. Decorate with any pastry trimmings if liked. Glaze with beaten egg. Place on a flan dish.

Combination bake at 180°C using 30% (low) microwave power for 40 minutes, removing the greaseproof paper after 20 minutes and glazing the sides of the pie with beaten egg. Allow to cool.

To make the jellied stock, sprinkle the gelatine over the stock and allow to soften. Microwave at 100% (high) for ½ minute until clear and dissolved. Pour the jellied stock through the hole in the pie lid and chill to set.

Serve cold with salad – delicious on picnics, for summer fêtes, harvest suppers and wedding breakfasts.

Variation:

Raised game and chicken pie

Prepare and cook as above but use 450g/1lb chopped game meat instead of the bacon. Season with chopped mixed herbs to taste.

Microwave only fresh and frozen fish and shellfish cooking guide

Cod

STEAMED COD STEAKS Fold or tuck in the end flaps of the cod steaks and secure into a neat shape with wooden cocktail sticks. Arrange in a large dish with sticks to the centre. Dot with a little butter and sprinkle with a little lemon juice. Cover with vented cling film and cook for time specified, rotating dish twice. Leave to stand, covered, for 2–3 minutes before serving.

Quantity	Power	Minutes
2 × 225g/8oz	100% (high)	5
4 × 225g/8oz	100% (high)	8–9

STEAMED COD FILLETS Arrange the fish fillets in a large dish with the thicker portions to the outside of the dish. Dot with a little butter, sprinkle with lemon juice and season with pepper. Cover with vented cling film and cook for the time specified, rearranging once. Leave to stand, covered, for 3 minutes before serving.

Quantity	Power	Minutes
450g 1lb	100% (high)	5–7

POACHED COD FILLETS Arrange the cod fillets in a large dish with the thicker portions to the outside of the dish. Season with pepper and lemon juice and pour over milk, water or stock. Cover with vented cling film and cook for the time specified, rearranging once. Leave to stand, covered, for 3 minutes before serving.

Quantity	Liquid	Power	Minutes
450g/1lb	8 tbsp	100% (high)	5–7

FROZEN COD STEAKS To thaw, place in a dish, cover and

cook for the time specified, turning over or rearranging once. Leave to stand for 10 minutes before using.

Quantity	Power	Minutes
1 × 225g/8oz	20% (defrost)	2–2½
2 × 225g/8oz	20% (defrost)	3–4
4 × 225g/8oz	20% (defrost)	6–7

FROZEN COD FILLETS To thaw, place in a dish with thicker portions to outer edge. Cover and cook for the time specified, rearranging once. Leave to stand for 5 minutes before using.

Quantity	Power	Minutes
450g/1lb	20% (defrost)	7–8

Crabmeat

FROZEN TO THAW Leave in wrappings. Cook for the time and power specified, turning over once. Leave to stand for 2 minutes then flake to use.

Quantity	Power	Minutes
225g/8oz	20% (defrost)	4

Fish roes

TO COOK FRESH Place rinsed, soft fish roes (herring, for example) into a small dish with melted butter and salt and pepper to taste. Cover and cook for the time specified, stirring once. Leave to stand, covered, for 2 minutes before serving.

Quantity	Butter	Power	Minutes
100g/4oz	1 tbsp	30% (low)	4–4½
225g/8oz	2 tbsp	30% (low)	6–8

Haddock

STEAMED HADDOCK STEAKS Fold or tuck in the end flaps of the haddock steaks and secure into a neat shape with wooden cocktail sticks. Arrange, with sticks to the centre, in a large dish. Dot with a little butter and sprinkle with a little lemon juice. Cover with vented cling film and cook for the time specified, rotating dish twice. Leave to stand, covered, for 2–3 minutes before serving.

Quantity	Power	Minutes
2 × 225g/8oz	100% (high)	5
4 × 225g/8oz	100% (high)	8–9

STEAMED HADDOCK FILLETS   Arrange the fish fillets in a large dish with the thicker portions to the outside. Dot with a little butter, sprinkle with lemon juice and season with pepper. Cover with vented cling film and cook for the time specified, rearranging once. Leave to stand, covered, for 3 minutes before serving.

Quantity	Power	Minute
450g/1lb	100% high	5–7

POACHED HADDOCK FILLETS   Arrange the fillets in a large dish with the thicker portions to the outside. Season with pepper and lemon juice and pour over milk, water or stock. Cover with vented cling film and cook for the time specified, rearranging once. Leave to stand, covered, for 3 minutes before serving.

Quantity	Liquid	Power	Minutes
450g/1lb	8 tbsp	100% high	5–7

FROZEN HADDOCK STEAKS   To thaw, place in a dish, cover and cook for the time specified, turning over or rearranging once. Leave to stand for 10 minutes before using.

Quantity	Power	Minutes
1 × 225g/8oz	20% defrost	2–2½
2 × 225g/8oz	20% defrost	3–4
4 × 225g/8oz	20% defrost	6–7

FROZEN HADDOCK FILLETS   To thaw, place in a dish with thicker portions to outer edge. Cover and cook for the time specified, rearranging once. Leave to stand for 5 minutes before using.

Quantity	Power	Minutes
450g/1lb	20% (defrost)	7–8

Halibut

STEAMED HALIBUT STEAKS Fold or tuck in the end flaps of the halibut steaks and secure into a neat shape with wooden cocktail sticks. Arrange, with sticks to the centre, in a large dish. Dot with a little butter and sprinkle with a little lemon juice. Cover with vented cling film and cook for the time specified, rotating dish twice. Leave to stand, covered, for 2–3 minutes before serving.

Quantity	Power	Minutes
2 × 225g/8oz	100% (high)	4–5
4 × 225g 8oz	100% (high)	7½–8

FROZEN HALIBUT STEAKS To thaw, place in a dish, cover and cook for the time specified, turning over or rearranging once. Leave to stand for 10 minutes before using.

Quantity	Power	Minutes
1 × 225g/8oz	20% (defrost)	2–2½
2 × 225g/8oz	20% (defrost)	3–4
4 × 225g/8oz	20% (defrost)	6–7

Herring

TO COOK FRESH Remove heads and clean and gut. Slash the skin in 2 to 3 places to prevent bursting. Shield the tail end with a little foil if preferred. Place in a dish or on a roasting rack, season with salt, pepper and lemon juice if preferred, and cover with greaseproof paper. Cook for the calculated time according to weight, turning and rearranging once. Leave to stand, covered, for 2–3 minutes before serving.

Quantity	Power	Minutes
per 450g/1lb	100% (high)	3–4

FROZEN WHOLE HERRING   To thaw, place on a roasting rack or in a shallow dish and cook for the calculated time according to weight, turning over once. Leave to stand for 10 minutes before using.

Quantity per 450g/1lb	Power	Minutes
	20% (defrost)	5-7

Kippers

FRESH   Remove heads and tails using scissors. Place, skin-side down, on a plate. Cover loosely and cook for the time specified, rearranging once.

Quantity	Power	Minutes
1	100% (high)	1-2
2	100% (high)	3-4
4	100% (high)	6-7

FROZEN KIPPER FILLETS   To thaw and cook, place the frozen cook-in-bag on a plate and snip a couple of vents in the bag. Cook for the time specified, turning over once.

Quantity	Power	Minutes
1 × 175g/6oz packet	100% (high)	5-6

Lobster

TO REHEAT COOKED WHOLE LOBSTER AND LOBSTER TAILS   Place in a cooking dish and cover with vented cling film. Cook for the time specified, turning over once. Leave to stand for 5 minutes before serving or using.

Quantity	Power	Minutes
450g/1lb whole	100% (high)	6-8
450g/1lb tails	100% (high)	5-6

Mackerel

TO COOK FRESH   Remove heads and clean and gut. Slash the skin in 2 to 3 places to prevent bursting. Shield the tail-end with a little foil if preferred. Place in a dish or on a roasting rack, season with salt, pepper and lemon juice as desired, and cover with greaseproof paper. Cook for the calculated time according to weight, turning and rearranging once. Leave to stand, covered, for 2–3 minutes before serving.

Quantity	Power	Minutes
per 450g/1lb	100% (high)	3–4

FROZEN WHOLE MACKEREL To thaw, place on a roasting rack or in a shallow dish and cook for the calculated time according to weight, turning over once. Leave to stand for 10 minutes before using.

Quantity	Power	Minutes
per 450g/1lb	20% (defrost)	5–7

Mussels

FRESH Scrub or brush and scrape, wash thoroughly and place in a large cooking dish with the water (or white wine if preferred). Cover loosely and cook for the time specified, stirring once. Remove with a slotted spoon, discarding any mussels that do not open.

Quantity	Water	Power	Minutes
675g/1½lb	75ml/3fl oz	100% (high)	5

Plaice

BRAISED/POACHED PLAICE FILLETS Place a few slices of carrot, celery, onion and lemon in a large shallow dish with a bay leaf and 50ml/2fl oz water. Cover loosely with vented cling film. Cook for the first time specified. Add the fish fillets with the thicker portions to the outer edge of the dish. Re-cover and cook for the second time specified, rearranging and rotating once. Leave to stand, covered, for 5 minutes before serving.

168

Quantity	Power	1st time	2nd time
550g/1¼lb	100% high	4–6 minutes	5–7½ minutes

STEAMED PLAICE FILLETS   Arrange the fish fillets in a large dish with the thicker portions to the outside of the dish. Dot with a little butter, sprinkle with lemon juice and season with pepper. Cover with vented cling film and cook for the time specified, rearranging once. Leave to stand, covered, for 3 minutes before serving.

Quantity	Power	Minutes
450g/1lb	100% (high)	4–6

FROZEN PLAICE FILLETS   To thaw, place in a dish with the thicker portions to the outer edge. Cover and cook for the time specified, rearranging once. Leave to stand for 5 minutes before using.

Quantity	Power	Minutes
450g/1lb	20% (defrost)	7–8

FROZEN WHOLE PLAICE   To thaw, place on a plate. Cover and cook for the time specified, shielding the tail-end with a little foil halfway through cooking as necessary. Leave to stand for 3 minutes before using.

Quantity	Power	Minutes
1 × 275g/10oz	20% (defrost)	4–6
2 × 275g/10oz	20% (defrost)	10–12

Prawns and shrimps

FRESH UNCOOKED   Place rinsed prawns in a dish with water, a bayleaf and a dash of vinegar. Cover tightly with vented cling film. Cook for the time specified, stirring once. Leave to stand, covered, for 3 minutes. Drain and cool quickly.

Quantity	Water	Power	Minutes
450g/1lb	600ml/1 pint	100% (high)	6–8
900g/2lb	600ml/1 pint	100% (high)	8–10

FROZEN COOKED   To thaw, place in a dish and cook for the time specified, stirring twice.

Quantity	Power	Minutes
450g/1lb	20% (defrost)	7–8

Red or grey mullet

FRESH WHOLE   Arrange the cleaned and gutted mullet in a shallow dish. Slash the skin in 2 to 3 places to prevent bursting and sprinkle with a little lemon juice if desired. Cover and cook for the time specified, rearranging the fish or turning the dish once. Leave to stand, covered, for 5 minutes before serving.

Quantity	Power	Minutes
2 × 200–250g/7–9oz	100% (high)	3–5
4 × 200–250g/7–9oz	100% (high)	7–9

FROZEN WHOLE   To thaw, place in a shallow dish and cook for the time specified, turning or rearranging twice. Leave to stand for 5 minutes before using.

Quantity	Power	Minutes
2 × 200–250g/7–9oz	20% (defrost)	9–11
4 × 200–250g/7–9oz	20% (defrost)	19–21

Red snapper

TO COOK WHOLE FRESH   Season scaled and gutted fish inside and out and place or wrap in a buttered greaseproof paper 'parcel'. Place on a baking dish and cook for the time specified, rearranging once. Leave to stand, covered, for 5 minutes before serving with a sauce as desired.

Quantity	Power	Minutes
2 × 450–550g/1–1½lb	100% (high)	6–9

FROZEN WHOLE   To thaw individually (for best results), place in a shallow dish, cover and cook for the time specified, turning over once. Rinse in cold water then dry to use.

170

Quantity	Power	Minutes
1 × 450–550g/1–1½lb	50% (medium)	2½–3½

Salmon and salmon trout

FRESH SALMON STEAKS   Arrange the salmon steaks in a shallow dish so that the tail-ends are to the centre of the dish. Brush with a little melted butter or sprinkle with a little lemon juice and herbs if desired. Cover with greaseproof paper and cook for the time specified, rearranging or turning once. Leave to stand for 5 minutes before serving.

Quantity	Power	Minutes
2 × 225g/8oz	100% (high)	2–2½
4 × 225g/8oz	100% (high)	4–5
or 4 × 175g/6oz	50% (medium)	9–10

TO COOK WHOLE SALMON OR SALMON TROUT   Prick the salmon skin in several places to prevent bursting and place in a shallow cooking dish. Add a little lemon juice and boiling water to moisten. Cover with greaseproof paper or vented cling film and cook for the time specified, rotating the dish 3 times. Leave to stand, covered, for 5 minutes before serving.

Quantity	Power	Minutes
1 × 450g/1lb	100% (high)	6–8
1 × 900g/2lb	100% (high)	10–14
1 × 1.5kg/3lb	100% (high)	15–19
1 × 1.8kg/4lb	100% (high)	20–22

FROZEN SALMON STEAKS   To thaw, place in a shallow dish, cover and cook for the time specified, turning over and rearranging once. Leave to stand, covered, for 5–10 minutes before using.

Quantity	Power	Minutes
2 × 225g/8oz	20% (defrost)	4–5
4 × 225g/8oz	20% (defrost)	10–12
4 × 175g/6oz	20% (defrost)	10

FROZEN WHOLE SALMON OR SALMON TROUT   To thaw, place
in a shallow dish, cover and cook for the time specified,
turning over and rotating the dish twice. Shield the head
and tail with a little foil as necessary. Leave to stand,
covered, for 5–10 minutes before using.

Quantity	Power	Minutes
1 × 450g/1lb	20% (defrost)	6–8
1 × 900g/2lb	20% (defrost)	12–16
1 × 1.5kg/3lb	20% (defrost)	18–20
1 × 1.8kg/4lb	20% (defrost)	22–24

Scallops

FRESH   Place in a shallow dish. Cover with dampened
absorbent kitchen towel and cook for the time specified,
rearranging once. Leave to stand, covered, for 3 minutes
before using or serving.

Quantity	Power	Minutes
450g/1lb	100% (high)	4–6
or 450g/1lb	50% (medium)	8–12

FROZEN   Place in a bowl, cover and cook for the time
specified, stirring and breaking apart twice. Leave to stand,
covered, for 5 minutes before using.

Quantity	Power	Minutes
1 × 350g/12oz packet	20% (defrost)	6–8
450g/1lb	20% (defrost)	7½–10

Scampi

FRESH UNCOOKED   Place rinsed, shelled scampi in a dish
with water, a bayleaf and a dash of vinegar. Cover with
vented cling film. Cook for the time specified, stirring once.
Leave to stand, covered, for 3 minutes. Drain and use
quickly.

Quantity	Water	Power	Minutes
450g/1lb	600ml/1 pint	100% (high)	6–8
900g/2lb	600ml/1 pint	100% (high)	8–10

FROZEN COOKED   To thaw, place in a dish and cook for the time specified, stirring twice.

Quantity	Power	Minutes
450g/1lb	20% (defrost)	7–8

Smoked haddock

STEAMED SMOKED HADDOCK FILLETS   Arrange the fish fillets in a large dish with the thicker portions to the outside of the dish. Dot with a little butter, sprinkle with a little lemon juice and season with salt and pepper if preferred. Cover with vented cling film and cook for the time specified, rearranging once. Leave to stand, covered, for 3 minutes before serving.

Quantity	Power	Minutes
450g/1lb	100% (high)	5–6

POACHED SMOKED HADDOCK FILLETS   Arrange the smoked haddock fillets in a large dish with the thicker portions to the outside of the dish. Season with pepper and lemon juice if preferred, and pour over water or milk. Cover with vented cling film and cook for the time specified, rearranging once. Leave to stand, covered, for 3 minutes before serving.

Quantity	Liquid	Power	Minutes
450g/1lb	8 tbsp	100% (high)	5–6

FROZEN SMOKED HADDOCK FILLETS   To thaw and cook, place the frozen cook-in-bag on a plate and snip a couple of vents in the bag. Cook for the time specified, turning over once.

Quantity	Power	Minutes
1 × 175g/6oz packet	100% (high)	5–6

Sole

BRAISED/POACHED SOLE FILLETS   Place a few slices of carrot, celery, onion and lemon in a large shallow dish with a bayleaf and 50ml/2fl oz water. Cover loosely with vented cling film. Cook for the first time specified. Add the fish fillets with the thicker portions to the outer edge of the dish. Re-cover and cook for the second time specified, rearranging and rotating once. Leave to stand, covered, for 5 minutes before serving.

Quantity	Power	1st time	2nd time
550g/1¼lb	100% (high	4–6 minutes	5–7½ minutes

STEAMED SOLE FILLETS Arrange the fish fillets in a large dish with the thicker portions to the outside of the dish. Dot with a little butter, sprinkle with lemon juice and season with pepper. Cover with vented cling film and cook for the time specified, rearranging once. Leave to stand, covered, for 3 minutes before serving.

Quantity	Power	Minutes
450g/1lb	100% (high)	4–6

FROZEN SOLE FILLETS To thaw, place in a dish with thicker portions to the outer edge. Cover and cook for the time specified, rearranging once. Leave to stand for 5 minutes before using.

Quantity	Power	Minutes
450g/1lb	20% (defrost)	7–8

Trout

FRESH WHOLE Arrange the cleaned and gutted trout in a shallow dish. Slash the skin in 2 to 3 places to prevent bursting and sprinkle with a little lemon juice if preferred. Cover and cook for the time specified, rearranging or turning the dish once. Leave to stand, covered, for 5 minutes before serving.

Quantity	Power	Minutes
2 × 225–275g/8–10oz	100% (high)	3–5
4 × 225–275g/8–10oz	100% (high)	7–9

FROZEN WHOLE To thaw, place in a shallow dish and cook

for the time specified, turning or rearranging twice. Leave to stand for 5 minutes before using.

Quantity	Power	Minutes
2 × 225–275g/8–10oz	20% (defrost)	9–11
4 × 225–275g/8–10oz	20% (defrost)	19–21

Whitebait

FROZEN To thaw, place in a dish, cover and cook for the time specified, breaking gently apart. Leave to stand for 10–15 minutes before using.

Quantity	Power	Minutes
225g/8oz	20% (defrost)	5–7

Whiting

BRAISED/POACHED WHITING FILLETS Place a few slices of carrot, celery, onion and lemon in a large shallow dish with a bayleaf and 50ml/2fl oz water. Cover loosely with vented cling film. Cook for the first time specified. Add the fish fillets with the thicker portions to the outer edge of the dish. Re-cover and cook for the second time specified, rearranging and rotating once. Leave to stand, covered, for 5 minutes before serving.

Quantity	Power	1st time	2nd time
550g/1¼lb	100% (high)	4–6 minutes	5–7½ minutes

STEAMED WHITING FILLETS Arrange the fish fillets in a large dish with the thicker portions to the outside of the dish. Dot with a little butter, sprinkle with lemon juice and season with pepper. Cover with vented cling film and cook for the time specified, rearranging once. Leave to stand, covered, for 3 minutes before serving.

Quantity	Power	Minutes
450g/1lb	100% (high)	4–6

FROZEN WHITING FILLETS To thaw. place in a dish with

thicker portions to the outer edge. Cover and cook for the time specified, rearranging once. Leave to stand for 5 minutes before using.

Quantity	Power	Minutes
450g/1lb	20% (defrost)	7–8

Microwave only pasta and rice cooking guide

Pasta

PRE-COOKING LASAGNE FOR LAYERING WITH MEAT
MIXTURE   Place lasagne in a large rectangular dish with
the boiling water and a pinch of salt. Cover and cook for
the time specified, rearranging the sheets once. Drain and
rinse under cold running water to use.

Quantity	Water	Power	Minutes
225g/8oz	750ml/1¼ pints	100% (high)	7–9

PRE-COOKING CANNELLONI FOR STUFFING   Place the
cannelloni in a dish and add the boiling water and a pinch
of salt. Cover and cook for the time specified. Leave to stand
for 5 minutes then drain and stuff and cover with chosen
sauce.

Quantity	Water	Power	Minutes
225g/8oz	750ml/1¼ pints	100% (high)	1

FRESH PASTA (all types)   Place pasta in a large dish with a
little oil and the boiling water. Cover and cook for the time
specified. Drain and use as required.

Quantity	Water	Power	Minutes
225g/8oz	750ml/1¼ pints	100% (high)	2–3

CANNED PASTA   Place canned pasta (macaroni cheese,
ravioli in tomato sauce, spaghetti in tomato sauce or pasta
shapes in sauce, for example) in a bowl, cover and cook for
the time specified, stirring once.

Quantity	Power	Minutes
1 × 213g/7½oz can	100% (high)	1½–2
1 × 397g/14oz can	100% (high)	2½–3
1 × 425g/15oz can	100% (high)	2½–3

DRIED PASTA   Place the pasta in a large bowl with the boiling water and a little oil. Cook for the time specified, stirring once. Leave to stand for 3–5 minutes before draining to serve.

Quantity	Water	Power	Minutes
225g/8oz egg noodles and tagliatelle	1.2 litres/2 pints	100% (high)	6
225g/8oz short-cut macaroni	1.2 litres/2 pints	100% (high)	10
225g/8oz pasta shells and shapes	1.2 litres/2 pints	100% (high)	12–14
225g/8oz spaghetti	1.2 litres/2 pints	100% (high)	10–12
225g/8oz ravioli	1.5 litres/2½ pints	100% (high)	10

FROZEN COOKED PASTA   To thaw and reheat, place in a dish, cover and cook for the time specified, stirring twice.

Quantity	Power	Minutes
275g/10oz	20% (defrost)	10

Rice

LONG-GRAIN WHITE   Place in a large cooking dish with boiling water, salt and a knob of butter, if preferred. Cover loosely with a lid or vented cling film and cook for first time and power setting. Reduce power setting and cook for second time specified, stirring twice. Leave to stand, covered, for 5 minutes before serving. Fluff the rice with a fork to separate to serve.

Quantity	Water	Salt	1st Time/Power	2nd Time/Power
100g/4oz	300ml/½ pint	½ tsp	3 minutes/ 100% (high)	12 minutes/ 50% (medium)
150g/5oz	350ml/12 fl oz	½ tsp	3 minutes/ 100% (high)	12 minutes/ 50% (medium)
175g/6oz	400ml/14fl oz	½ tsp	3 minutes/ 100% (high)	12 minutes/ 50% (medium)
200g/7oz	475ml/16fl oz	¾ tsp	3 minutes/ 100% (high)	12 minutes/ 50% (medium)

225g/8oz	550ml/18fl oz	1 tsp	3 minutes/ 100% (high)	12 minutes/ 50% (medium)
275g/10oz	600ml/1 pint	1 tsp	3 minutes/ 100% (high)	12 minutes/ 50% (medium)

LONG-GRAIN BROWN   Place in a large cooking dish with boiling water, salt and a knob of butter, if preferred. Cover loosely with a lid or vented cling film and cook for first time and power setting. Reduce power setting and cook for second time specified, stirring 2–3 times. Leave to stand, covered, for 5 minutes before serving. Fluff the rice with a fork to separate to serve.

Quantity	Water	Salt	1st Time/Power	2nd Time/Power
100g/4oz	300ml/½ pint	½ tsp	3 minutes/ 100% (high)	25 minutes/ 50% (medium)
150g/5oz	350ml/12fl oz	½ tsp	3 minutes/ 100% (high)	25 minutes 50% (medium)
175g/6oz	400ml/14fl oz	½ tsp	3 minutes/ 100% (high)	25 minutes/ 50% (medium)
200g/7oz	475ml/16fl oz	¾ tsp	3 minutes/ 100% (high)	25 minutes/ 50% (medium)
225g/8oz	550ml/18fl oz	1 tsp	3 minutes/ 100% (high)	25 minutes/ 50% (medium)
275g/10oz	600ml/1 pint	1 tsp	3 minutes/ 100% (high)	25 minutes/ 50% (medium)

LONG-GRAIN AND WILD RICE MIX   Place in a large cooking dish with boiling water, salt and a knob of butter. Cover loosely with a lid or vented cling film and cook for first time and power setting. Reduce power setting and cook for second time specified, stirring twice. Leave to stand, covered, for 5 minutes before serving. Fluff the rice mixture with a fork to separate to serve.

Quantity	Water	Salt	1st Time/Power	2nd Time/Power
1 × 400g/ 14oz packet	700ml/24fl oz	1 tsp	3 minutes/ 100% (high)	12 minutes/ 50% (medium)

FROZEN COOKED RICE   To thaw and reheat, place in a dish,

cover and cook for the time specified. stirring twice. Leave
to stand, covered. for 2 minutes before using.

Quantity	Power	Minutes
225g/8oz	100% (high,	5–6
450g/1lb	100% high)	7–8

WILD RICE   Soak the rice in 600ml/1 pint warm water for
2–3 hours. Drain thoroughly. Place in a bowl with the oil,
boiling water and seasonings to taste. Cover and cook for
the time specified, stirring once. Leave to stand, covered,
for 5 minutes before serving.

Quantity	Oil	Water	Power	Minutes
100g. 4oz	1 tbsp	600ml 1 pint	100% (high.	30

Microwave only grain, bean and dried pulse cooking guide

Grains

Barley

POT BARLEY   Toast if preferred. Place in a large cooking dish with boiling water and salt. Cover loosely with a lid or vented cling film and cook for first time and power setting. Reduce power setting and cook for second time specified, stirring 3 times. Leave to stand, covered, for 5–10 minutes before serving. Fluff with a fork to separate the grains to serve.

Quantity	Water	Salt	1st Time/Power	2nd Time/Power
175g/6oz	1 litre/1¾ pints	1 tsp	3 minutes/ 100% (high)	40 minutes/ 50% (medium)

Buckwheat

PRE-ROASTED   Place in a large cooking dish with boiling water and salt. Cover loosely with a lid or vented cling film and cook for first time and power setting. Reduce power setting and cook for second time specified, stirring 2–3 times. Leave to stand, covered, for 3–5 minutes before serving. Fluff with a fork to separate and serve.

Quantity	Water	Salt	1st Time/Power	2nd Time/Power
175g/6oz	600ml/1 pint	1 tsp	3 minutes/ 100% (high)	12 minutes/ 50% (medium)

Bulghur

BULGHUR GRAINS (CRACKED WHEAT) Place in a large
cooking dish with boiling water and salt. Cover loosely
with a lid or vented cling film and cook for first time and
power setting. Reduce power setting and cook for second time
specified, stirring twice. Leave to stand, covered, for 3–5
minutes before serving. Fluff the grains with a fork to
separate and serve.

Quantity	Water	Salt	1st Time/Power	2nd Time/Power
225g/8oz	500ml/18fl oz	1 tsp	3 minutes/ 100% (high)	9–12 minutes/ 50% (medium)

Couscous

PRE-COOKED Place in a cooking dish with warm water.
Leave to soak for 10 minutes. Add butter and salt to taste.
Cook for time specified, stirring every 3–4 minutes. Leave
to stand, covered, for 2–3 minutes before serving.

Quantity	Water	Butter	Power	Minutes
350g/12oz (to serve 4)	250ml/8fl oz	50g/2oz	50% (medium)	15

Millet

MILLET GRAINS Toast if liked. Place in a large cooking dish
with boiling water and salt. Cover loosely with a lid or
vented cling film and cook for first time and power setting.
Reduce power setting and cook for second time and power
setting, stirring twice. Leave to stand, covered, for 3–5
minutes before serving. Fluff with a fork to separate the
grains to serve.

Quantity	Water	Salt	1st Time/Power	2nd Time/Power
225g/8oz	650ml/22fl oz	1 tsp	3 minutes/ 100% (high)	12 minutes/ 50% (medium)

Oats

OAT GRAINS   Toast if preferred. Place in a large cooking
dish with boiling water and salt. Cover loosely with a lid
or vented cling film and cook for first time and power setting.
Reduce power setting and cook for second time specified,
stirring twice. Leave to stand, covered, for 5–10 minutes
before serving. Fluff the grains with a fork to separate to
serve.

Quantity	Water	Salt	1st Time/Power	2nd Time/Power
175g/6oz	750ml/1¼ pints	1 tsp	3 minutes/ 100% (high)	20–22 minutes/ 50% (medium)

Rye

RYE GRAINS   Soak overnight or for 6–8 hours. Place in a
large cooking dish with boiling water and salt. Cover
loosely with a lid or vented cling film and cook for first time
and power setting. Reduce power setting and cook for second
time specified stirring 3 times. Leave to stand. covered, for
5–10 minutes before serving. Fluff the grains with a fork
to separate to serve.

Quantity	Water	Salt	1st Time/Power	2nd Time/Power
175g/6oz	750ml/1¼ pints	1 tsp	3 minutes/ 100% (high)	40 minutes/ 50% (medium)

Wheat

WHEAT GRAINS   Soak overnight, or for 6–8 hours. Place in
a large cooking dish with boiling water and salt. Cover
loosely with a lid or vented cling film and cook for first time
and power setting. Reduce power setting and cook for second
time specified, stirring 3 times. Leave to stand. covered, for
5–10 minutes before serving. Fluff the wheat grains with a
fork to separate to serve.

Quantity	Water	Salt	1st Time/Power	2nd Time/Power
175g/6oz	1 litre/1¾ pints	1 tsp	3 minutes/ 100% (high)	40 minutes/ 50% (medium)

Dried beans and peas

ADUKI BEANS, BLACKEYE BEANS, WHOLE DRIED GREEN PEAS AND PINTO BEANS Place soaked beans or peas in a cooking dish. Cover with boiling water. Cover and cook for the first time and power specified. Reduce the power setting and cook for the second time specified, adding extra boiling water to cover if needed. Drain to use as required.

Quantity soaked beans	1st Time/Power	2nd Time/Power
225g/8oz	10 minutes/ 100% (high)	10–15 minutes/ 50% (medium)

BLACK BEANS, BROAD BEANS, BUTTER OR LIMA BEANS, CANNELLINI BEANS, CHICK PEAS, FLAGEOLET BEANS, HARICOT BEANS, RED KIDNEY BEANS AND ROSE COCOA OR BORLOTTI BEANS Place soaked beans or peas in a cooking dish. Cover with boiling water. Cover and cook for the first time and power specified. Reduce the power setting and cook for the second time specified, adding extra boiling water to cover if needed. Drain to use as required.

Quantity soaked beans	1st Time/Power	2nd Time/Power
225g/8oz	10 minutes/ 100% (high)	20–25 minutes/ 50% (medium)

SPLIT PEAS Place soaked peas in a cooking dish. Cover with boiling water. Cover and cook for the time specified.

Quantity soaked peas	Power	Minutes
225g/8oz	100% (high)	10

LENTILS Place in a large dish with a little chopped onion, celery and lemon juice. Cover with boiling water or stock and salt and pepper to taste. Cover and cook for the time specified, stirring once. Time cooking according to end use.

Quantity lentils	Water	Power	Minutes
225g/8oz	900ml/1½ pints	100% (high)	20–25

(Note: To hasten soaking prior to cooking: Place in a cooking dish, cover with boiling water. Cover and cook for 5 minutes at 100% (high). Leave to stand for 1½ hours before draining and rinsing to cook.)

Index

Index compiled by Peva Keane

Arto der Haroutunian
The Whole Grain Cookbook £4.95

Pilav dishes of the world

A wealth of healthy and imaginative eating that draws on the most time-honoured culinary tradition of mankind.

All the world's ancient civilisations were based on grain . . . wheat and barley in the Middle East and Europe, rice in China and Japan, maize in the Americas, sorghum and millet in Africa. In those distant days, grain was prepared by roasting or boiling in water or milk. In time, other ingredients were added to enrich the flavour, create variety, and produce a more nourishing dietary balance.

Thus was created one of the greatest foods of all – the pilav . . . *pilao, pollo, risotto, paella, kasha* . . . all grain dishes cooked with herbs, spices, vegetables, nuts, fruits, meat, poultry and fish.

Arto der Haroutunian has gathered together over 150 recipes, from the popular *paella* and the simple buckwheat and butter *kasha* to the extravagant rice dishes of India and Iran; mouth-watering ideas for your kitchen drawn from the four corners of the earth. His pages are enriched with invaluable information about the different grains and spiced with evocative myths and proverbs.

A PAN ORIGINAL

Carol Bowen
A–Z of Microwave Cookery £3.99

How to cook absolutely everything
Revised and expanded edition

A practical reference guide to cooking basic foods in a microwave.

Whether you want to thaw meat, cook frozen peas, ripen cheese or melt chocolate, you can save time by using your microwave.

Carol Bowen, an expert in microwave cookery, has spent years testing basic items which are suitable for cooking the microwave way. The result is the *A–Z of Microwave Cookery*, now fully revised and expanded to cover almost 200 basic foods, arranged alphabetically from almonds to yogurt.

Information is at your fingertips with a useful glossary of terms, a guide to temperature settings, and precise instructions on:

Preparing food for the oven
Covering, turning and stirring during cooking
Power settings and cooking times according to weight.

The indispensable at-a-glance guide to fast, efficient cooking.

Also available in Pan by Carol Bowen:

The Microwave Cookbook

A PAN ORIGINAL

All Pan books are available at your local bookshop or newsagent, or can be ordered direct from the publisher. Indicate the number of copies required and fill in the form below.

Send to: **CS Department, Pan Books Ltd., P.O. Box 40, Basingstoke, Hants.   RG21 2YT.**

or phone: 0256 469551 (Ansaphone), quoting title, author and Credit Card number.

Please enclose a remittance* to the value of the cover price plus: 60p for the first book plus 30p per copy for each additional book ordered to a maximum charge of £2.40 to cover postage and packing.

*Payment may be made in sterling by UK personal cheque, postal order, sterling draft or international money order, made payable to Pan Books Ltd.

Alternatively by Barclaycard/Access:

Card No.   ☐☐☐☐☐☐☐☐☐☐☐☐☐☐☐☐☐

Signature:

Applicable only in the UK and Republic of Ireland.

While every effort is made to keep prices low, it is sometimes necessary to increase prices at short notice. Pan Books reserve the right to show on covers and charge new retail prices which may differ from those advertised in the text or elsewhere.

NAME AND ADDRESS IN BLOCK LETTERS PLEASE:

....

Name ——————————————————————————————

Address ——————————————————————————————

——————————————————————————————————

——————————————————————————————————

——————————————————————————————————

3/87